Summer Bridge
Grades 2

Editor: Sandra Toland
Layout Design: Tiara Reynolds
Inside Illustrations: Nathan Aaron, Mike Duggins, Ray Lambert, Wayne Miller
Cover Design: Chasity Rice
Cover Illustration: Wayne Miller

Printed in the USA • All rights reserved.   ISBN 978-1-60022-451-5

Table of Contents

How to Use This Book

The *Summer Bridge Math* series is designed to help children improve their mathematical skills during the summer months and between grades. *Summer Bridge Math* includes several extra components to help make your child's study of mathematics easier and more inviting.

For example, an **Assessment** test has been included to help you determine your child's mathematical knowledge and what skills need improvement. Use this test, as well as the **Assessment Analysis**, as a diagnostic tool for those areas in which your child may need extra practice.

Furthermore, the **Incentive Contract** will motivate your child to complete the work in *Summer Bridge Math*. Together, you and your child choose the reward for completing specific sections of the book. Check off the pages that your child has completed, and he or she will have a record of his or her accomplishment.

Examples are included for each new skill that your child will learn. The examples are located in red boxes at the top of the pages. On each page, the directions refer to the example your child needs to complete a specific type of activity.

Assessment

Write each numeral.

A. seven _____   nineteen _____   thirty-seven _____

seventy _____   sixty-five _____

What is the value of:

B. 6 in 612? _____   4 in 241? _____   9 in 9,243? _____

C. 342 equals _____ hundreds _____ tens _____ ones

D. 819 equals _____ hundreds _____ tens _____ ones

E. 2,345 equals _____ thousands _____ hundreds _____ tens _____ ones

Use <, >, or = to compare the numerals.

F. 35 _____ 71   10 _____ 3   91 _____ 94   68 _____ 88

Solve the problems.

G.
$$\begin{array}{r} 21 \\ +\ 42 \end{array} \qquad \begin{array}{r} 64 \\ +\ 12 \end{array} \qquad \begin{array}{r} 86 \\ +\ 11 \end{array} \qquad \begin{array}{r} 59 \\ +\ 19 \end{array} \qquad \begin{array}{r} 73 \\ +\ 17 \end{array}$$

H.
$$\begin{array}{r} 49 \\ -\ 37 \end{array} \qquad \begin{array}{r} 83 \\ -\ 13 \end{array} \qquad \begin{array}{r} 77 \\ -\ 41 \end{array} \qquad \begin{array}{r} 40 \\ -\ 16 \end{array} \qquad \begin{array}{r} 54 \\ -\ 27 \end{array}$$

I.
$$\begin{array}{r} 12 \\ \times\ 2 \end{array} \qquad \begin{array}{r} 7 \\ \times\ 6 \end{array} \qquad \begin{array}{r} 79 \\ \times\ 7 \end{array} \qquad \begin{array}{r} 8 \\ \times\ 2 \end{array} \qquad \begin{array}{r} 32 \\ \times\ 8 \end{array}$$

J. $7\overline{)49}$ $5\overline{)35}$ $4\overline{)28}$ $6\overline{)38}$ $8\overline{)25}$

Summer Bridge Math RB-904087

Write the equations for each fact family.

K. 2, 4, 8

_____ X _____ = _____

_____ X _____ = _____

_____ ÷ _____ = _____

_____ ÷ _____ = _____

L. 5, 6, 30

_____ X _____ = _____

_____ X _____ = _____

_____ ÷ _____ = _____

_____ ÷ _____ = _____

Write the time shown on each clock.

M.

_____ : _____   _____ : _____

Count the money. Write how much.

N.

_____

Write the fractions. Then, use <, >, or = to compare.

O.

_____   _____

P.

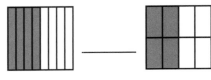

_____   _____

Write the name of each shape.

Q.

_____   _____   _____   _____

Solve each problem.

R. The soccer team scored 6 goals each game. They played 3 games. How many goals did they score? _____ goals

S. Sam's family has 12 cookies. There are 4 people in Sam's family. How many cookies will each person get? _____ cookies

Summer Bridge Math RB-904087

Assessment Analysis

Assessment Answer Key

A. 7, 19, 37, 70, 65
B. 600, 40, 9,000
C. 3, 4, 2
D. 8, 1, 9
E. 2, 3, 4, 5
F. <, >, <, <
G. 63, 76, 97, 78, 90
H. 12, 70, 36, 24, 27
I. 24, 42, 553, 16, 256

J. 7, 7, 7, 6 r2, 3 r1
K. Answers may be in a different order.
$2 \times 4 = 8$, $4 \times 2 = 8$,
$8 \div 4 = 2$, $8 \div 2 = 4$
L. Answers may be in a different order.
$5 \times 6 = 30$, $6 \times 5 = 30$,
$30 \div 6 = 5$, $30 \div 5 = 6$

M. 4:35, 8:26
N. $7.77
O. $\frac{4}{6} > \frac{3}{6}$
P. $\frac{4}{8} = \frac{4}{8}$
Q. trapezoid, cylinder, parallelogram, circle
R. 18 goals
S. 3 cookies

After reviewing the Assessment test, match the problems answered incorrectly to the corresponding activity pages. Your child should spend extra time on those activities to strengthen his or her math skills.

Diagnostic Problem	Review Section	Review Pages
A., B., C., D., E., F.	Numeration	7–18
G., H.	Addition and Subtraction	19–34
I., J., K., L.	Multiplication and Division	35–51
M., N.	Time and Money	52–58
O., P.	Fractions and Decimals	63–73
Q.	Geometry	74–80
R., S.	Problem Solving	84–92

Incentive Contract

Numeration		√	My Incentive Is:
7	Naming Numbers in Word Form		
8	Naming Larger Numbers in Word Form		
9	Reading Number Words Practice		
10	Ordinal Numbers		
11	Place Value		
12	Place Value Practice		
13	Writing in Expanded Form		
14	Writing in Standard Form		
15	Comparing the Values of Numerals		
16	Comparing Numerals Practice		
17	Rounding to the Nearest Hundred		
18	Skip Counting		

Addition		√	My Incentive Is:
19	Two-Digit Addition		
20	Two-Digit Addition with Regrouping		
21	Three-Digit Addition		
22	Three-Digit Addition with Regrouping		
23	Four-Digit Addition		
24	Column Addition		
25	Adding Money		

Subtraction		√	My Incentive Is:
26	Two-Digit Subtraction		
27	Two-Digit Subtraction with Regrouping		
28	Three-Digit Subtraction		
29	Three-Digit Subtraction with Regrouping		
30	Four-Digit Subtraction		
31	Subtraction with Regrouping Practice		

Mixed Addition and Subtraction		√	My Incentive Is:
32	Two-Digit Mixed Practice		
33	Three-Digit Mixed Practice		
34	Out of This World!		

Multiplication		√	My Incentive Is:
35	Introduction to Multiplication		
36	Multiplication Chart		
37	Finding the Facts		
38	Multiplication Practice		
39	Two-Digit Multiplication		
40	Two-Digit Multiplication with Regrouping		
41	Three-Digit Multiplication		
42	Multiplying Money		

Division		√	My Incentive Is:
43	Introduction to Division		
44	Understanding Division		
45	Using Division Signs		
46	Dividing by a Single-Digit Numeral		
47	Division with Remainders		
48	Division Practice		

Mixed Multiplication and Division		√	My Incentive Is:
49	Connecting Operations		
50	Fact Families		
51	Mixed Practice		

Time and Money		√	My Incentive Is:
52	Telling Time		
53	Five-Minute Intervals		
54	Drawing Hands on Clocks		
55	Introduction to Money		
56	Skip Counting Coins		
57	Counting Money		
58	Calculating Change		

Measurement		√	My Incentive Is:
59	Standard Measurement		
60	Comparing Linear Measurements		
61	Increments and Weight		
62	Capacity and Temperature		

Fractions and Decimals		√	My Incentive Is:
63	Introduction to Fractions		
64	Equivalent Fractions		
65	Comparing Fractions		
66	Adding and Subtracting Fractions		
67	Improper Fractions		
68	Sequencing Decimals		
69	Using Decimals		
70	Adding and Subtracting Decimals		
71	Tenths		
72	Tenths Practice		
73	Place Value Practice		

Patterns and Geometry		√	My Incentive Is:
74	Predicting Patterns		
75	Number Patterns		
76	Patterns and Functions		
77	Shapes		
78	Spatial Figures		
79	Lines of Symmetry		
80	Perimeter		

Statistics and Graphs		√	My Incentive Is:
81	Exploring Probability		
82	Reading a Chart		
83	Interpreting Graphs and Grids		

Problem Solving		√	My Incentive Is:
84	Addition and Subtraction		
85	Three-Digit Addition and Subtraction		
86	Multiplication		
87	Choosing the Operation		
88	Division		
89	Division with Remainders		
90	Time		
91	Money		
92	Problem Solving Using Charts		

Naming Numbers in Word Form

Numbers can be written as words, as well as numerals. Below are the words for the numerals 0 through 12.

0–zero	1–one	2–two	3–three	4–four
5–five	6–six	7–seven	8–eight	9–nine
10–ten	11–eleven	12–twelve		

Study the word names above. Then, find the written name for each numeral. Use the matching letters to answer the question.

Where does the male emperor penguin keep the eggs warm?

$$\overline{}\ \overline{} \qquad \overline{}\ \overline{}\ \overline{}$$
74   19   46   93   36

$$\overline{}\ \overline{}\ \overline{}\ \overline{}\ \overline{}$$
21   52   76   62   85

ninety-three	I	sixty-two	T	forty-six	H
fifty-nine	R	seventy-four	O	fifty-two	E
nineteen	N	eighty-five	!	twenty-one	F
seventy-six	E	thirty-six	S	ninety	V

Summer Bridge Math RB-904087

Naming Larger Numbers in Word Form

You can use **place value** columns to help you write numbers in word form. They look like this:

H	T	O
6	4	1

= six hundred forty-one

Th	H	T	O
3	2	1	8

= three thousand two hundred eighteen

Study the examples above. Then, read each number's name in word form. Color its matching number on the chicken or on the egg.

A. six thousand nine hundred eleven

B. four thousand seventy-three

C. nine thousand two hundred seven

D. eight hundred thirty-nine

E. nine thousand six hundred one

F. eight thousand three hundred ninety

G. four hundred seventeen

H. five thousand eighty-two

I. four hundred seventy

J. three thousand five hundred twelve

K. six thousand nine hundred fourteen

417   9,207   839

3,512   6,911   6,914

9,601   4,073   5,082

470   4,413   8,390

L. What numeral is left over? _____

8

Reading Number Words Practice

> This number is **seven hundred forty-three**. Do not use the word "and" when writing or saying large numbers.

743

Study the examples on page 8. Then, draw lines to match the numerals with the number words.

A.	347	five hundred nine
B.	279	nine hundred ninety-nine
C.	960	three hundred forty-seven
D.	719	nine hundred sixty
E.	801	one hundred thirty-five
F.	590	six hundred eighty
G.	135	two hundred seventy-nine
H.	509	seven hundred nineteen
I.	680	eight hundred one
J.	999	five hundred ninety

Write the numeral that means the same as each number word.

K. three hundred thirteen _____

L. eight hundred nine _____

M. four hundred twenty-six _____

N. two hundred eleven _____

O. seven hundred fifty-one _____

P. one hundred five _____

Q. five hundred thirty-two _____

R. nine hundred forty-four _____

Summer Bridge Math RB-904087

Ordinal Numbers

The **ordinal number** of an object is found by counting its place in line. To count ordinal numbers, use first (1st), second (2nd), third (3rd), etc.

Write the missing numbers on the tickets to show their order. Then, use the tickets to help you find the answers to the questions.

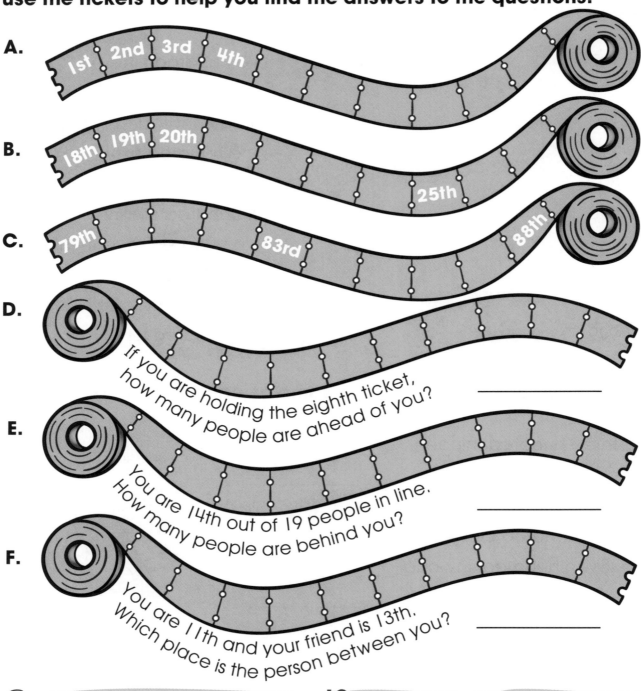

A. 1st 2nd 3rd 4th

B. 18th 19th 20th 25th

C. 79th 83rd 88th

D. If you are holding the eighth ticket, how many people are ahead of you? _____

E. You are 14th out of 19 people in line. How many people are behind you? _____

F. You are 11th and your friend is 13th. Which place is the person between you? _____

Place Value

I thousand, 2 hundreds, 3 tens, 2 ones is equal to the number 1,232. We say "one thousand two hundred thirty-two."

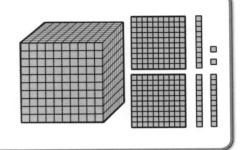

__1__ thousand __2__ hundreds __3__ tens __2__ ones = __1,232__

Study the example above. Then, write how many thousands, hundreds, tens, and ones. Write the total.

A.

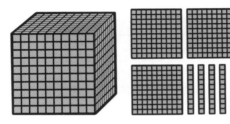

_____ thousands _____ hundreds

_____ tens _____ ones = _____

B.

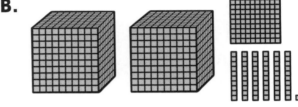

_____ thousands _____ hundreds

_____ tens _____ ones = _____

C.

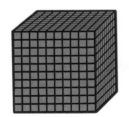

_____ thousands _____ hundreds

_____ tens _____ ones = _____

D.

_____ thousands _____ hundreds

_____ tens _____ ones = _____

E.

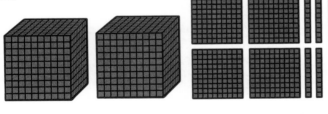

_____ thousands _____ hundreds

_____ tens _____ ones = _____

F.

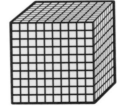

_____ thousands _____ hundreds

_____ tens _____ ones = _____

Place Value Practice

Study the example on page 11. Then, write the number of ten thousands, thousands, hundreds, tens, and ones in each numeral below.

	Ten Thousands	Thousands	Hundreds	Tens	Ones

A. 5,739
B. 14,650
C. 27,381
D. 40,736
E. 91,475
F. 55,837
G. 86,902
H. 4,560
I. 31,048
J. 11,111
K. 79,277
L. 68,593
M. 99,999
N. 48,305

What place value does each circled numeral represent?

O. 3,④56 _____   90,②86 _____

P. ⑦,394 _____   ④7,519 _____

Q. ①6,321 _____   38,1②7 _____

R. 25,0④7 _____   ⑧4,031 _____

S. 39,⑤86 _____   7②,797 _____

T. 58,72⑨ _____   59,3⑥8 _____

U. 40,3⑦0 _____   30,58④ _____

V. ⑦2,532 _____   ⑧6,395 _____

W. 9⑥,411 _____   39,⑤86 _____

Summer Bridge Math RB-904087

Writing in Expanded Form

The place value system is based on **groups of ten**. This chart shows how the thousands, hundreds, tens, and ones relate to each other.

1,000	100	10	1
1 thousand = 10 hundreds	1 hundred = 10 tens	1 ten = 10 ones	

This chart is helpful when writing numbers in expanded form.

$$3,649 = 3,000 + 600 + 40 + 9$$

Study the example above. Then, write each number in expanded form.

		Thousands	Hundreds	Tens	Ones
A.	9,516 =		+	+	+
B.	2,358 =		+	+	+
C.	1,407 =		+	+	+
D.	921 =		+	+	+
E.	7,800 =		+	+	+
F.	3,264 =		+	+	+
G.	5,182 =		+	+	+
H.	614 =		+	+	+
I.	4,073 =		+	+	+
J.	9,530 =		+	+	+

13

Summer Bridge Math RB-904087

Writing in Standard Form

Study the example on page 13. Then, write the numeral that means the same as each expanded number.

A. 1,000 + 500 + 30 + 3 = _____

B. 5,000 + 900 + 40 + 7 = _____

C. 3,000 + 700 + 50 + 5 = _____

D. 7,000 + 400 + 70 + 9 = _____

E. 9,000 + 20 + 1 = _____

F. 3,000 + 100 + 2 = _____

G. 3,000 + 500 + 6 = _____

H. 6,000 + 90 + 8 = _____

I. 3,000 + 600 + 9 = _____

J. 1,000 + 600 + 90 + 8 = _____

Write the number in expanded form.

K. 3,456 _____

L. 7,324 _____

M. 9,152 _____

N. 3,569 _____

O. 2,431 _____

P. 4,022 _____

Summer Bridge Math RB-904087

Comparing the Values of Numerals

The arrow points to the smaller number and opens wide to the larger number. 64 > 62 means that 64 is **greater than** 62.

=	>	<
means equal to	means greater than	means less than

Study the example above. Then, use >, <, or = to compare each set of numerals.

A.   72   [   ]   27

B.   61   [   ]   60

C.   34   [   ]   43

D.   27   [   ]   27

E.   23   [   ]   32

F.   98   [   ]   96

G.   82   [   ]   83

H.   56   [   ]   65

I.   18   [   ]   18

J.   49   [   ]   50

15

Comparing Numerals Practice

Circle the numeral that is the least.

A.	173	149	156	206	347	165
B.	699	943	943	878	566	903
C.	510	430	530	770	680	820
D.	390	745	845	691	759	425
E.	941	812	852	814	916	804

Circle the numeral that is the most.

F.	746	981	873	699	870	847
G.	633	709	599	671	433	598
H.	695	768	845	871	555	796
I.	493	561	664	793	990	889
J.	567	765	675	783	623	805

Use greater than (>) and less than (<) signs to compare numerals.

K. 439 _____ 670   944 _____ 872

L. 730 _____ 750   610 _____ 603

M. 567 _____ 576   887 _____ 891

N. 991 _____ 919   499 _____ 500

O. 635 _____ 471   781 _____ 902

P. 1000 _____ 998   549 _____ 798

Q. 473 _____ 374   895 _____ 958

R. 768 _____ 391   399 _____ 405

S. 818 _____ 881   914 _____ 941

Summer Bridge Math RB-904087

Rounding to the Nearest Hundred

When **rounding** to the nearest hundred, use these rules:
1. Look at the tens place.
2. If the number in the tens place is 0, 1, 2, 3, or 4, round down.
3. If the number in the tens place is 5, 6, 7, 8, or 9, round up.

You have discovered a hidden treasure! Study the rules above for rounding. Then, estimate the value in each treasure chest. Round these amounts to the nearest hundred.

$692 $700

$140 $

$569 $

$303 $

$684 $

$851 $

$712 $

$476 $

$925 $

Skip Counting

Skip counting means following a given pattern as you count. You are probably used to counting by twos, fives, and tens. Use the number line to "skip" the given number of times.

Count by fives.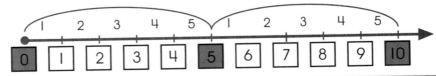

Study the example above. Then, color the number boxes to show skip counting.

A. Start at 0 and count by fours.

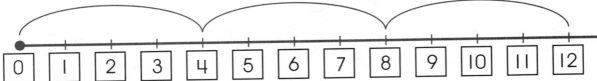

B. Start at 0 and count by sixes.

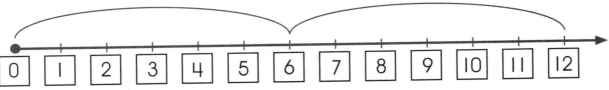

C. Start at 33 and count by threes.

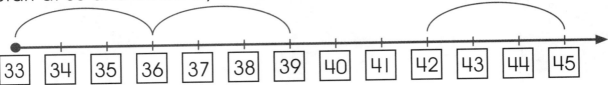

D. Start at 62 and count by twos.

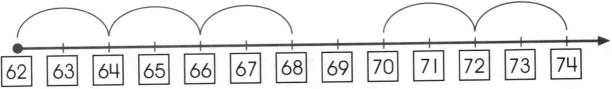

E. Start at 84 and count by fours.

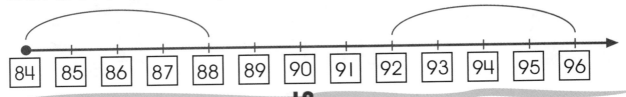

Summer Bridge Math RB-904087

Two-Digit Addition

<table>
<tr><td>1. Add the ones column.
Five plus 3 equals 8.</td><td>2. Add the tens column.
Two plus 1 equals 3.</td></tr>
<tr><td><pre> 2**5**
+ 1**3**
   8</pre></td><td><pre>**2**5
+ **1**3
38</pre></td></tr>
</table>

Study the example above. Then, solve each problem.

A.

23	64	47	13	55	16
+ 42	+ 25	+ 31	+ 45	+ 30	+ 53

B.

70	82	74	58	26	35
+ 29	+ 11	+ 23	+ 41	+ 33	+ 54

C.

12	83	41	19	22	36
+ 77	+ 13	+ 37	+ 60	+ 37	+ 23

D.

15	18	84	27	46	20
+ 72	+ 81	+ 12	+ 62	+ 41	+ 51

E.

52	75	24	51	29	25
+ 36	+ 10	+ 43	+ 27	+ 50	+ 61

F.

31	47	19	62	33	43
+ 55	+ 32	+ 30	+ 37	+ 52	+ 31

Summer Bridge Math RB-904087

Two-Digit Addition with Regrouping

1. Add the ones column. Eight plus 4 equals 12. **Regroup** to the tens column.	2. Add the tens column. Six plus 2 plus 1 equals 9.
$\begin{array}{r} {}^1 \\ 6\,\mathbf{8} \\ +\,2\,\mathbf{4} \\ \hline \mathbf{2} \end{array}$	$\begin{array}{r} {}^1 \\ \mathbf{6}\,8 \\ +\,\mathbf{2}\,4 \\ \hline \mathbf{9}\,2 \end{array}$

Study the example above. Then, solve each problem.

A.

27	39	46	57	49	63
+ 24	+ 53	+ 35	+ 29	+ 15	+ 27

B.

75	93	58	64	86	47
+ 19	+ 37	+ 34	+ 28	+ 17	+ 28

C.

66	79	43	56	98	81
+ 26	+ 32	+ 27	+ 58	+ 32	+ 59

D.

64	57	34	25	18	27
+ 17	+ 26	+ 49	+ 36	+ 28	+ 59

E.

43	26	27	53	33	49
+ 27	+ 36	+ 69	+ 37	+ 48	+ 27

Summer Bridge Math RB-904087

Three-Digit Addition

1. Add the ones column. Two plus 4 equals 6.	2. Add the tens column. Six plus 3 equals 9.	3. Add the hundreds column. Four plus 1 equals 5.
46**2** + 1 3 **4** **6**	4 **6** 2 + 1 **3** 4 **9** 6	**4** 6 2 + **1** 3 4 **5** 9 6

Study the example above. Then, solve each problem.

A.
$$182 + 703$$ $$231 + 547$$ $$825 + 163$$ $$436 + 562$$ $$325 + 202$$

B.
$$274 + 320$$ $$641 + 345$$ $$908 + 61$$ $$365 + 424$$ $$207 + 712$$

C.
$$352 + 436$$ $$475 + 510$$ $$724 + 143$$ $$650 + 227$$ $$298 + 500$$

D.
$$525 + 261$$ $$631 + 155$$ $$447 + 432$$ $$319 + 450$$ $$752 + 136$$

E.
$$933 + 52$$ $$547 + 131$$ $$830 + 69$$ $$626 + 331$$ $$487 + 411$$

F.
$$631 + 325$$ $$488 + 211$$ $$562 + 407$$ $$723 + 166$$ $$506 + 353$$

Three-Digit Addition with Regrouping

Once you know how to add three-digit numbers, you can add any size numbers together. Remember: always start with the ones column and work your way through the columns to the left.

Study the example on page 20. Then, solve each problem.

A.

283	497	176	325	651
+ 168	+ 205	+ 640	+ 867	+ 179

B.

304	517	237	482	117
+ 519	+ 334	+ 807	+ 531	+ 488

C.

624	431	329	772	532
+ 276	+ 382	+ 682	+ 405	+ 489

D.

136	479	379	386	670
+ 477	+ 342	+ 483	+ 364	+ 259

E.

823	937	736	648	462
+ 357	+ 468	+ 136	+ 246	+ 369

F.

837	689	350	427	601
+ 337	+ 285	+ 261	+ 367	+ 289

Four-Digit Addition

Study the examples on pages 19–21. Then, solve each problem.

A.

3,261	4,639	7,216	5,952	1,794
+ 5,239	+ 2,073	+ 2,593	+ 3,128	+ 2,607

B.

2,773	9,076	6,415	4,701	8,213
+ 3,535	+ 3,970	+ 1,765	+ 6,354	+ 1,529

C.

3,257	9,935	1,224	6,597	4,165
+ 4,809	+ 1,260	+ 8,967	+ 3,212	+ 7,042

D.

7,309	3,295	5,716	6,907	8,813
+ 4,597	+ 4,305	+ 1,708	+ 4,132	+ 2,076

E.

1,943	2,967	3,846	6,381	5,490
+ 3,065	+ 7,120	+ 2,195	+ 5,436	+ 6,327

F.

8,361	5,639	1,735	2,465	9,675
+ 4,209	+ 2,076	+ 3,291	+ 3,637	+ 2,404

Summer Bridge Math RB-904087

Column Addition

First, add the first 2 numbers. Two plus 7 equals 9.
Then, add the last number. Nine plus 4 equals 13.

$$
\begin{array}{r} 2 \\ 7 \\ + 4 \\ \hline \end{array} \rightarrow \begin{array}{r} 9 \\ + 4 \\ \hline 13 \end{array}
$$

Study the example above. Then, solve each problem.

A.

1	4	3	7	2	1	6
3	2	4	1	8	9	5
+ 2	+ 1	+ 2	+ 2	+ 1	+ 1	+ 1

B.

3	3	7	4	2	5	3
5	6	2	3	2	3	7
+ 4	+ 1	+ 4	+ 7	+ 3	+ 2	+ 2

C.

2	6	4	5	7	9	8
8	4	4	5	7	4	7
+ 3	+ 3	+ 3	+ 5	+ 3	+ 1	+ 3

D.

5	4	2	7	8	6	3
3	8	9	5	2	2	3
4	2	1	3	5	2	4
+ 1	+ 1	+ 3	+ 3	+ 3	+ 8	+ 3

E.

3	4	9	6	7	8	1
7	8	1	6	8	3	8
5	2	5	3	1	0	2
+ 1	+ 3	+ 2	+ 3	+ 2	+ 2	+ 7

Summer Bridge Math RB-904087

Adding Money

To find the sum of several numbers, use the same steps as before:
1. Add the ones column. Regroup if necessary.
2. Add the tens column. Regroup if necessary.
3. Add the hundreds column. Regroup if necessary.
4. Add the thousands column.

When adding money, be sure to include the **decimal point** and the **dollar sign** in your answer.

Which is the richest kingdom? Study the examples on pages 20, 21, and 24. Then, solve each problem. Be sure to include the money symbols. Color the answers on the castles. The first castle to be completely shaded is in the richest kingdom!

$13.50

$6.63

$10.58

$12.70

$13.34

$7.07

A.
```
   $1.36
    2.07
 +  3.64
   $7.07
```
```
   $6.77
    3.52
 +  1.08
```
```
   $2.09
    0.33
 +  9.81
```

$16.53

$12.38

B.
```
   $3.07
    4.12
 +  6.31
```
```
   $0.94
    8.41
 +  7.18
```
```
   $1.46
    3.72
 +  5.40
```

$11.37

C.
```
   $3.73
    3.19
 +  6.42
```
```
   $7.17
    8.01
 +  2.90
```
```
   $4.36
    5.56
 +  9.12
```

$18.08

D.
```
   $5.71
    0.09
 +  0.83
```
```
   $1.80
    9.84
 +  1.06
```

$12.23

$19.04

Summer Bridge Math RB-904087

Two-Digit Subtraction

1. Subtract the ones column. Six minus 2 equals 4.	2. Subtract the tens column. Three minus 1 equals 2.
3**6** − 1**2** **4**	**3**6 − **1**2 **2**4

Study the example above. Then, solve each problem.

A.
$$\begin{array}{r} 86 \\ -32 \end{array}$$
$$\begin{array}{r} 52 \\ -12 \end{array}$$
$$\begin{array}{r} 67 \\ -45 \end{array}$$
$$\begin{array}{r} 95 \\ -30 \end{array}$$
$$\begin{array}{r} 87 \\ -26 \end{array}$$
$$\begin{array}{r} 48 \\ -33 \end{array}$$

B.
$$\begin{array}{r} 39 \\ -13 \end{array}$$
$$\begin{array}{r} 66 \\ -46 \end{array}$$
$$\begin{array}{r} 38 \\ -14 \end{array}$$
$$\begin{array}{r} 75 \\ -52 \end{array}$$
$$\begin{array}{r} 88 \\ -37 \end{array}$$
$$\begin{array}{r} 74 \\ -24 \end{array}$$

C.
$$\begin{array}{r} 47 \\ -15 \end{array}$$
$$\begin{array}{r} 96 \\ -73 \end{array}$$
$$\begin{array}{r} 58 \\ -54 \end{array}$$
$$\begin{array}{r} 81 \\ -21 \end{array}$$
$$\begin{array}{r} 57 \\ -33 \end{array}$$
$$\begin{array}{r} 49 \\ -25 \end{array}$$

D.
$$\begin{array}{r} 36 \\ -14 \end{array}$$
$$\begin{array}{r} 87 \\ -77 \end{array}$$
$$\begin{array}{r} 70 \\ -30 \end{array}$$
$$\begin{array}{r} 65 \\ -50 \end{array}$$
$$\begin{array}{r} 99 \\ -73 \end{array}$$
$$\begin{array}{r} 28 \\ -12 \end{array}$$

E.
$$\begin{array}{r} 97 \\ -25 \end{array}$$
$$\begin{array}{r} 64 \\ -23 \end{array}$$
$$\begin{array}{r} 72 \\ -22 \end{array}$$
$$\begin{array}{r} 89 \\ -55 \end{array}$$
$$\begin{array}{r} 55 \\ -14 \end{array}$$
$$\begin{array}{r} 83 \\ -20 \end{array}$$

Summer Bridge Math RB-904087

Two-Digit Subtraction with Regrouping

1. Subtract the ones column. You cannot subtract 7 from 2, so regroup.	2. To regroup, take 1 ten from the 4 tens, leaving 3 tens. Add the ten to the ones to make 12 ones. Subtract. Twelve minus 7 equals 5.	3. Subtract the tens column. Three tens minus 2 tens equals 1 ten.
$$\begin{array}{r} 4\,\mathbf{2} \\ -\ 2\,\mathbf{7} \\ \hline \end{array}$$	$$\begin{array}{r} \overset{3}{4}\,{}^{1}2 \\ -\ 2\ 7 \\ \hline \mathbf{5} \end{array}$$	$$\begin{array}{r} \overset{3}{4}\,{}^{1}2 \\ -\ \mathbf{2}\ 7 \\ \hline \mathbf{1}\ 5 \end{array}$$

Study the example above. Then, solve each problem.

A.

$$\begin{array}{r} 36 \\ -17 \\ \hline \end{array} \qquad \begin{array}{r} 98 \\ -19 \\ \hline \end{array} \qquad \begin{array}{r} 28 \\ -\ 9 \\ \hline \end{array} \qquad \begin{array}{r} 41 \\ -15 \\ \hline \end{array} \qquad \begin{array}{r} 33 \\ -17 \\ \hline \end{array} \qquad \begin{array}{r} 67 \\ -18 \\ \hline \end{array}$$

B.

$$\begin{array}{r} 72 \\ -53 \\ \hline \end{array} \qquad \begin{array}{r} 85 \\ -27 \\ \hline \end{array} \qquad \begin{array}{r} 43 \\ -29 \\ \hline \end{array} \qquad \begin{array}{r} 96 \\ -37 \\ \hline \end{array} \qquad \begin{array}{r} 64 \\ -36 \\ \hline \end{array} \qquad \begin{array}{r} 50 \\ -18 \\ \hline \end{array}$$

C.

$$\begin{array}{r} 47 \\ -19 \\ \hline \end{array} \qquad \begin{array}{r} 94 \\ -26 \\ \hline \end{array} \qquad \begin{array}{r} 75 \\ -39 \\ \hline \end{array} \qquad \begin{array}{r} 61 \\ -22 \\ \hline \end{array} \qquad \begin{array}{r} 33 \\ -19 \\ \hline \end{array} \qquad \begin{array}{r} 82 \\ -35 \\ \hline \end{array}$$

D.

$$\begin{array}{r} 71 \\ -46 \\ \hline \end{array} \qquad \begin{array}{r} 86 \\ -47 \\ \hline \end{array} \qquad \begin{array}{r} 94 \\ -35 \\ \hline \end{array} \qquad \begin{array}{r} 65 \\ -27 \\ \hline \end{array} \qquad \begin{array}{r} 92 \\ -44 \\ \hline \end{array} \qquad \begin{array}{r} 53 \\ -29 \\ \hline \end{array}$$

E.

$$\begin{array}{r} 76 \\ -38 \\ \hline \end{array} \qquad \begin{array}{r} 64 \\ -35 \\ \hline \end{array} \qquad \begin{array}{r} 76 \\ -27 \\ \hline \end{array} \qquad \begin{array}{r} 52 \\ -44 \\ \hline \end{array} \qquad \begin{array}{r} 83 \\ -25 \\ \hline \end{array} \qquad \begin{array}{r} 68 \\ -49 \\ \hline \end{array}$$

Three-Digit Subtraction

1. Subtract the ones column.	2. Subtract the tens column.	3. Subtract the hundreds column.
5 6 **4** − 1 3 **2** **2**	5 **6** 4 − 1 **3** 2 **3** 2	**5** 6 4 − **1** 3 2 **4** 3 2

Study the example above. Then, solve each problem.

A.
$$684 - 253$$
$$634 - 421$$
$$835 - 610$$
$$738 - 502$$
$$325 - 102$$

B.
$$874 - 321$$
$$647 - 325$$
$$958 - 146$$
$$363 - 242$$
$$567 - 362$$

C.
$$283 - 220$$
$$488 - 351$$
$$695 - 233$$
$$719 - 305$$
$$894 - 752$$

D.
$$975 - 342$$
$$767 - 425$$
$$836 - 132$$
$$547 - 235$$
$$658 - 510$$

E.
$$393 - 173$$
$$649 - 235$$
$$786 - 526$$
$$999 - 683$$
$$887 - 346$$

Summer Bridge Math RB-904087

Three-Digit Subtraction with Regrouping

1. Subtract the ones column. You cannot subtract 6 from 4, so regroup. Take 1 ten from the 3 tens. Add the ten to the ones to make 14 ones. Subtract.

$$\begin{array}{r} 5\overset{2}{\cancel{3}}\overset{1}{4} \\ -\ 2\ 5\ 6 \\ \hline 8 \end{array}$$

2. Look at the tens column. You cannot subtract 5 tens from 2 tens, so regroup. Take 1 hundred from the 5 hundreds. Add the hundred to the tens to make 12 tens. Subtract.

$$\begin{array}{r} \overset{4}{\cancel{5}}\overset{12}{\cancel{3}}\overset{1}{4} \\ -\ 2\ 5\ 6 \\ \hline 7\ 8 \end{array}$$

3. Subtract the hundreds column.

$$\begin{array}{r} \overset{4}{\cancel{5}}\overset{12}{\cancel{3}}\overset{1}{4} \\ -\ 2\ 5\ 6 \\ \hline 2\ 7\ 8 \end{array}$$

Study the example above. Then, solve each problem.

A.

837	516	825	713	624
− 138	− 247	− 356	− 284	− 367

B.

283	567	928	785	497
− 96	− 275	− 189	− 496	− 269

C.

553	476	764	676	952
− 129	− 138	− 335	− 227	− 344

D.

837	689	941	277	765
− 253	− 496	− 250	− 193	− 295

Summer Bridge Math RB-904087

Four-Digit Subtraction

Study the examples on pages 26–29. Then, solve each problem.

A.

9,375	2,772	3,943	5,814	5,932
− 4,969	− 1,476	− 1,876	− 2,867	− 3,845

B.

7,403	9,800	5,639	7,860	6,657
− 2,675	− 3,765	− 1,879	− 1,895	− 5,575

C.

8,207	9,730	7,796	3,905	5,667
− 4,648	− 4,698	− 2,994	− 1,847	− 2,909

D.

8,436	6,943	3,845	8,560	9,454
− 7,527	− 2,880	− 1,966	− 2,483	− 2,087

E.

7,571	5,965	4,739	7,430	8,956
− 3,875	− 1,879	− 3,465	− 2,767	− 3,979

Summer Bridge Math RB-904087

Subtraction with Regrouping Practice

subtraction

Study the examples on pages 26–29. Then, solve each problem.

A.
$$3,621 - 1,283$$
$$4,197 - 468$$
$$2,479 - 890$$
$$5,076 - 1,256$$

B.
$$9,616 - 758$$
$$3,804 - 1,192$$
$$8,941 - 173$$
$$982 - 497$$

C.
$$8,263 - 4,458$$
$$7,603 - 215$$
$$9,550 - 4,229$$
$$645 - 187$$

D.
$$850 - 76$$
$$2,972 - 493$$

Write your own subtraction problem that uses regrouping two times.

© Rainbow Bridge Publishing

Summer Bridge Math RB-904087

Two-Digit Mixed Practice

Study the examples on pages 19–20 and 26–27. Then, solve each problem.

A.

```
   87        29        51        26        35
 - 29      + 37      - 23      + 45      + 57
```

B.

```
   91        86        71        62        53
 - 67      - 27      - 52      + 19      - 21
```

C.

```
   47        84        31        93        44
 + 13      + 58      - 19      - 36      + 48
```

D.

```
   72        28        49        62        98
 - 39      + 57      - 31      + 25      - 37
```

E.

```
   88        29        77        66        11
 - 49      + 18      - 58      + 26      + 78
```

F.

```
   87        27        53        27        34
 + 26      + 47      - 34      + 55      - 18
```

Three-Digit Mixed Practice

Study the examples on pages 21–22 and 28–29. Then, solve each problem.

A.

$$187 + 838$$

$$492 - 185$$

$$886 + 340$$

$$725 + 287$$

$$630 - 168$$

B.

$$317 + 415$$

$$617 + 304$$

$$227 - 109$$

$$380 + 739$$

$$817 - 468$$

C.

$$374 - 176$$

$$537 + 285$$

$$620 - 182$$

$$972 + 409$$

$$732 - 269$$

D.

$$236 + 587$$

$$279 + 373$$

$$660 - 153$$

$$456 + 464$$

$$770 - 262$$

E.

$$803 - 377$$

$$917 - 458$$

$$746 + 336$$

$$548 + 476$$

$$476 + 389$$

F.

$$847 + 387$$

$$689 - 295$$

$$550 + 281$$

$$627 + 277$$

$$649 + 279$$

Out of This World!

Start from the center numeral and work out to solve each problem.

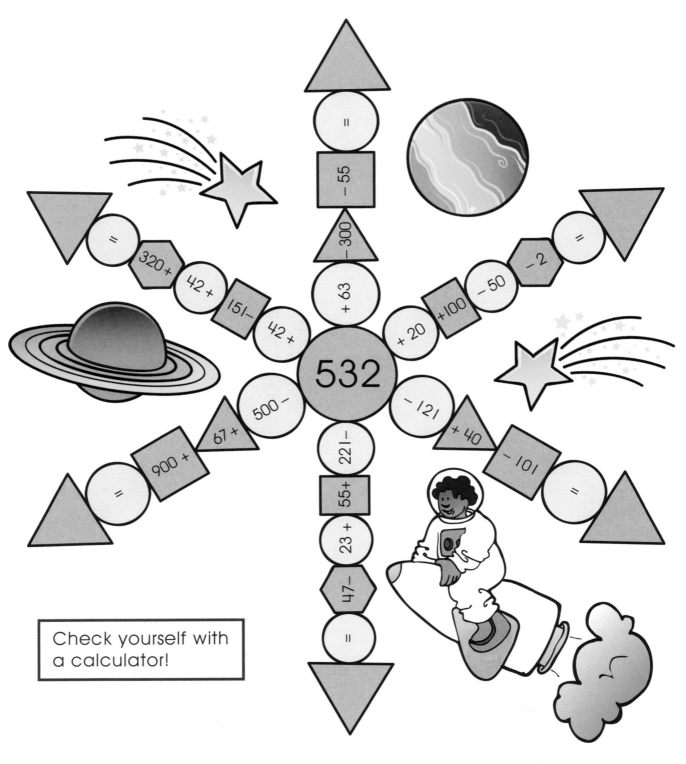

Check yourself with a calculator!

Summer Bridge Math RB-904087

To **multiply** means to use repeated addition. The answer to a multiplication problem is called the **product**. The numbers being multiplied are called **factors**. To more easily understand, imagine making equal groups. Then, add all of the groups together. Multiplication looks like this:

$4 + 4 + 4$

3 groups of 4

3×4 ← factors

12 ← product

Study the example above. Then, write an addition and multiplication problem for each picture. Find the sum and the product.

A.

× × × × ×
× × × × ×
× × × × ×

☐ + ☐ + ☐ = ☐

☐ × ☐ = ☐

B.

☆ ☆ ☆
☆ ☆ ☆

☐ + ☐ = ☐

☐ × ☐ = ☐

C.

☐ + ☐ + ☐ + ☐ = ☐

☐ × ☐ = ☐

D.

☐ + ☐ = ☐

☐ × ☐ = ☐

E.

× × ×
× × ×
× × ×

☐ + ☐ + ☐ = ☐

☐ × ☐ = ☐

F.

☐ + ☐ + ☐ = ☐

☐ × ☐ = ☐

G.

☐ + ☐ + ☐ = ☐

☐ × ☐ = ☐

H.

☐ + ☐ = ☐

☐ × ☐ = ☐

35

Summer Bridge Math RB-904087

Multiplication Chart

Complete the chart. Then, answer the questions.

x	1	2	3	4	5	6	7	8	9
1	1								
2									
3									
4									
5									
6									
7									
8									
9									

A. What does any number times 1 equal? _____

B. What pattern do you see in the twos?_____

_____

C. What pattern do you see in the fives? _____

_____

D. Add the digits for each answer in the nines. What number does each

answer equal? _____

E. 3 x 4 = 12. What does 4 x 3 equal?_____

Summer Bridge Math RB-904087

Finding the Facts

Study the example on page 35 or the multiplication chart on page 36. Then, find the product for each pair of factors below. Use the code to find the letters. Write the letters on the lines to answer the two riddles.

A	B	C	D	E	F	G	H	I	J	K	L	M	N	O	P	Q	R	S	T	U	V	W	X	Y	Z
64	4	42	7	24	16	0	18	40	11	19	49	59	25	12	13	21	56	8	54	32	28	45	60	9	14

What can you hold in your left hand but not in your right hand?

___ ___ ___ ___
3 x 3   6 x 2   8 x 4   7 x 8

___ ___ ___ ___ ___
8 x 7   5 x 8   1 x 0   6 x 3   6 x 9

___ ___ ___ ___ ___ !
8 x 3   7 x 7   2 x 2   3 x 4   9 x 5

Why is it so easy to weigh fish?

___ ___ ___ ___ ___ ___ ___
4 x 1   6 x 4   6 x 7   8 x 8   4 x 8   2 x 4   3 x 8

___ ___ ___ ___   ___ ___ ___ ___
4 x 4   8 x 5   1 x 8   9 x 2   3 x 6   8 x 8   7 x 4   4 x 6

___ ___ ___ ___ ___   ___ ___ ___
9 x 6   2 x 9   8 x 3   5 x 8   7 x 8   3 x 4   9 x 5   5 x 5

___ ___ ___ ___ ___ ___ !
4 x 2   7 x 6   8 x 8   7 x 7   6 x 4   8 x 1

Summer Bridge Math RB-904087

Multiplication Practice

Study the example on page 35. Then, solve each problem.

A.
$$\begin{array}{r} 2 \\ \times\, 2 \\ \hline \end{array}$$
$$\begin{array}{r} 3 \\ \times\, 2 \\ \hline \end{array}$$
$$\begin{array}{r} 5 \\ \times\, 3 \\ \hline \end{array}$$
$$\begin{array}{r} 1 \\ \times\, 6 \\ \hline \end{array}$$
$$\begin{array}{r} 6 \\ \times\, 2 \\ \hline \end{array}$$

B.
$$\begin{array}{r} 2 \\ \times\, 8 \\ \hline \end{array}$$
$$\begin{array}{r} 5 \\ \times\, 2 \\ \hline \end{array}$$
$$\begin{array}{r} 2 \\ \times\, 6 \\ \hline \end{array}$$
$$\begin{array}{r} 2 \\ \times\, 4 \\ \hline \end{array}$$
$$\begin{array}{r} 2 \\ \times\, 1 \\ \hline \end{array}$$

C.
$$\begin{array}{r} 7 \\ \times\, 2 \\ \hline \end{array}$$
$$\begin{array}{r} 3 \\ \times\, 6 \\ \hline \end{array}$$
$$\begin{array}{r} 9 \\ \times\, 2 \\ \hline \end{array}$$
$$\begin{array}{r} 8 \\ \times\, 2 \\ \hline \end{array}$$
$$\begin{array}{r} 4 \\ \times\, 5 \\ \hline \end{array}$$

D.
$$\begin{array}{r} 3 \\ \times\, 9 \\ \hline \end{array}$$
$$\begin{array}{r} 6 \\ \times\, 5 \\ \hline \end{array}$$
$$\begin{array}{r} 4 \\ \times\, 6 \\ \hline \end{array}$$
$$\begin{array}{r} 3 \\ \times\, 7 \\ \hline \end{array}$$
$$\begin{array}{r} 8 \\ \times\, 3 \\ \hline \end{array}$$

E.
$$\begin{array}{r} 4 \\ \times\, 4 \\ \hline \end{array}$$
$$\begin{array}{r} 5 \\ \times\, 6 \\ \hline \end{array}$$
$$\begin{array}{r} 5 \\ \times\, 8 \\ \hline \end{array}$$
$$\begin{array}{r} 7 \\ \times\, 9 \\ \hline \end{array}$$
$$\begin{array}{r} 8 \\ \times\, 8 \\ \hline \end{array}$$

F.
$$\begin{array}{r} 5 \\ \times\, 4 \\ \hline \end{array}$$
$$\begin{array}{r} 8 \\ \times\, 9 \\ \hline \end{array}$$
$$\begin{array}{r} 7 \\ \times\, 6 \\ \hline \end{array}$$
$$\begin{array}{r} 5 \\ \times\, 7 \\ \hline \end{array}$$
$$\begin{array}{r} 4 \\ \times\, 8 \\ \hline \end{array}$$

G.
$$\begin{array}{r} 6 \\ \times\, 6 \\ \hline \end{array}$$
$$\begin{array}{r} 7 \\ \times\, 4 \\ \hline \end{array}$$
$$\begin{array}{r} 8 \\ \times\, 7 \\ \hline \end{array}$$
$$\begin{array}{r} 9 \\ \times\, 9 \\ \hline \end{array}$$
$$\begin{array}{r} 9 \\ \times\, 4 \\ \hline \end{array}$$

H.
$$\begin{array}{r} 4 \\ \times\, 5 \\ \hline \end{array}$$
$$\begin{array}{r} 5 \\ \times\, 5 \\ \hline \end{array}$$
$$\begin{array}{r} 5 \\ \times\, 9 \\ \hline \end{array}$$
$$\begin{array}{r} 6 \\ \times\, 8 \\ \hline \end{array}$$
$$\begin{array}{r} 4 \\ \times\, 7 \\ \hline \end{array}$$

Two-Digit Multiplication

First, multiply the ones. Then, multiply the tens. Add.

$$\begin{array}{r} 1\,2 \\ \times\ \ 3 \\ \hline 6 \end{array}\ +\ \begin{array}{r} 1\,2 \\ \times\ \ 3 \\ \hline 3\,0 \end{array}\ =\ 36$$

Shortcut:

$$\begin{array}{r} 1\,2 \\ \times\ \ 3 \\ \hline 3\,6 \end{array}$$

Multiply the ones.
Multiply the tens.

Study the example above. Then, solve each problem.

A.

$$\begin{array}{r} 1\,2 \\ \times\ 4 \\ \hline \end{array} \qquad \begin{array}{r} 1\,1 \\ \times\ 2 \\ \hline \end{array} \qquad \begin{array}{r} 1\,3 \\ \times\ 2 \\ \hline \end{array} \qquad \begin{array}{r} 1\,3 \\ \times\ 3 \\ \hline \end{array}$$

B.

$$\begin{array}{r} 1\,1 \\ \times\ 3 \\ \hline \end{array} \qquad \begin{array}{r} 1\,4 \\ \times\ 2 \\ \hline \end{array} \qquad \begin{array}{r} 1\,2 \\ \times\ 3 \\ \hline \end{array} \qquad \begin{array}{r} 1\,1 \\ \times\ 4 \\ \hline \end{array}$$

C.

$$\begin{array}{r} 1\,3 \\ \times\ 1 \\ \hline \end{array} \qquad \begin{array}{r} 1\,1 \\ \times\ 6 \\ \hline \end{array} \qquad \begin{array}{r} 2\,2 \\ \times\ 3 \\ \hline \end{array} \qquad \begin{array}{r} 3\,2 \\ \times\ 2 \\ \hline \end{array}$$

D.

$$\begin{array}{r} 4\,2 \\ \times\ 2 \\ \hline \end{array} \qquad \begin{array}{r} 2\,4 \\ \times\ 2 \\ \hline \end{array} \qquad \begin{array}{r} 2\,2 \\ \times\ 2 \\ \hline \end{array} \qquad \begin{array}{r} 2\,1 \\ \times\ 3 \\ \hline \end{array}$$

E.

$$\begin{array}{r} 3\,3 \\ \times\ 3 \\ \hline \end{array} \qquad \begin{array}{r} 3\,2 \\ \times\ 3 \\ \hline \end{array} \qquad \begin{array}{r} 3\,1 \\ \times\ 3 \\ \hline \end{array} \qquad \begin{array}{r} 3\,1 \\ \times\ 2 \\ \hline \end{array}$$

Summer Bridge Math RB-904087

Two-Digit Multiplication with Regrouping

First, multiply the ones. Then, multiply the tens. Add.

$$\begin{array}{r} 1\,\mathbf{3} \\ \times\ \mathbf{6} \\ \hline 1\,\mathbf{8} \end{array} \quad + \quad \begin{array}{r} 1\,3 \\ \times\ \mathbf{6} \\ \hline \mathbf{6}\,\mathbf{0} \end{array} \;=\; \mathbf{78}$$

Shortcut:
Multiply the ones.
Regroup to the tens.

$$\begin{array}{r} {\scriptstyle 1} \\ 1\,3 \\ \times\ 6 \\ \hline \mathbf{7\,8} \end{array}$$

Multiply the tens.
$6 \times 10 = 60$
Add the extra ten.
$60 + 10 = 70$

Study the example above. Then, solve each problem.

A.
15	14	13	24	22
x 6	x 5	x 7	x 3	x 5

B.
12	25	32	23	14
x 7	x 4	x 6	x 7	x 8

C.
26	52	44	34	13
x 3	x 6	x 5	x 6	x 9

D.
84	45	32	16	28
x 3	x 6	x 9	x 7	x 2

E.
35	18	22	34	47
x 6	x 7	x 7	x 5	x 3

F.
19	33	42	63	83
x 2	x 6	x 8	x 4	x 5

Summer Bridge Math RB-904087

Three-Digit Multiplication

Study the examples on pages 39 and 40. Then, solve each problem.

A.
311	248	225	283	999	274
x 8	x 2	x 4	x 3	x 2	x 2

B.
143	215	103	150	103	208
x 7	x 3	x 8	x 5	x 9	x 4

C.
401	210	252	200	111	521
x 9	x 4	x 3	x 6	x 8	x 7

D.
411	517	108	162	136	510
x 9	x 6	x 8	x 4	x 3	x 7

E.
907	485	271	704	112	235
x 7	x 2	x 9	x 8	x 6	x 5

F.
362	125	422	891	107	790
x 3	x 8	x 4	x 6	x 9	x 5

Multiplying Money

When multiplying money, be sure to include the dollar sign and the decimal in your answer.

$$\begin{array}{r} \overset{5\ 2}{\$5.63} \\ \times\quad 8 \\ \hline \$45.04 \end{array} \qquad \begin{array}{r} \overset{5\ 1}{\$1.93} \\ \times\quad 6 \\ \hline \$11.58 \end{array}$$

Study the example above. Then, find the products. Be sure to include the dollar sign.

A.
$$\begin{array}{r} \$7.30 \\ \times\quad 5 \\ \hline \end{array} \qquad \begin{array}{r} \$3.41 \\ \times\quad 8 \\ \hline \end{array} \qquad \begin{array}{r} \$8.24 \\ \times\quad 3 \\ \hline \end{array} \qquad \begin{array}{r} \$6.15 \\ \times\quad 7 \\ \hline \end{array}$$

B.
$$\begin{array}{r} \$0.68 \\ \times\quad 2 \\ \hline \end{array} \qquad \begin{array}{r} \$1.98 \\ \times\quad 4 \\ \hline \end{array} \qquad \begin{array}{r} \$3.62 \\ \times\quad 6 \\ \hline \end{array} \qquad \begin{array}{r} \$2.99 \\ \times\quad 5 \\ \hline \end{array}$$

C.
$$\begin{array}{r} \$1.37 \\ \times\quad 7 \\ \hline \end{array} \qquad \begin{array}{r} \$0.91 \\ \times\quad 9 \\ \hline \end{array} \qquad \begin{array}{r} \$4.00 \\ \times\quad 8 \\ \hline \end{array} \qquad \begin{array}{r} \$1.23 \\ \times\quad 9 \\ \hline \end{array}$$

D.
$$\begin{array}{r} \$0.11 \\ \times\quad 8 \\ \hline \end{array} \qquad \begin{array}{r} \$3.82 \\ \times\quad 3 \\ \hline \end{array} \qquad \begin{array}{r} \$0.74 \\ \times\quad 4 \\ \hline \end{array} \qquad \begin{array}{r} \$6.80 \\ \times\quad 7 \\ \hline \end{array}$$

Summer Bridge Math RB-904087 © Rainbow Bridge Publishing

Introduction to Division

To **divide** means to make equal groups or to share equally. The answer to a division problem is called the **quotient**. Division looks like this:

Total   No. of   No. in
        groups   each
                 group

$12 \div 3 = 4$

Total   No. of   No. in
        groups   each
                 group

$10 \div 2 = 5$

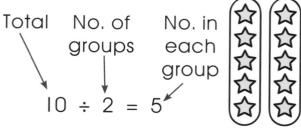

Study the examples above. Then, circle equal groups to find the quotient for each picture.

A.

$10 \div 5 = \boxed{}$

B.

$15 \div 3 = \boxed{}$

C.

$6 \div 3 = \boxed{}$

D.

$8 \div 2 = \boxed{}$

E.

$9 \div 3 = \boxed{}$

F.

$12 \div 4 = \boxed{}$

G.

$12 \div 6 = \boxed{}$

H.

$18 \div 3 = \boxed{}$

I.

$14 \div 7 = \boxed{}$

Understanding Division

> Twenty total objects are put into 4 groups. There are 5 objects in each group.
>
> $$20 \div 4 = 5$$
>
> 20 divided into 4 groups
>
>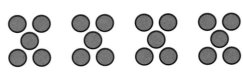
>
> $$4\overline{)20}^{\,5}$$

Study the examples above and on page 43. Then, solve each problem. Draw a picture. Write the equation.

A. 21 divided into 3 groups

_____

B. 30 divided into 5 groups

_____

C. 36 divided into 9 groups

_____

D. 18 divided into 6 groups

_____

Using Division Signs

We read this problem as
"12 **divided** by 3 **equals** 4."
Twelve put into 3 equal groups
equals 4 in each group.

$$12 \div 3 = \underline{\quad 4 \quad}$$

$$3\overline{)12}^{\,4}$$

Study the examples above and on pages 43 and 44. Then, solve each problem. Draw a picture.

A.
$$9 \div 3 = \underline{\quad\quad}$$

B.
$$8 \div 2 = \underline{\quad\quad}$$

C.
$$6 \div 2 = \underline{\quad\quad}$$

D.
$$16 \div 4 = \underline{\quad\quad}$$

E.
$$12 \div 6 = \underline{\quad\quad}$$

F.
$$18 \div 3 = \underline{\quad\quad}$$

Summer Bridge Math RB-904087

Dividing by a Single-Digit Numeral

Knowing your multiplication facts makes these division problems a snap!

Study the examples on pages 43–45. Then, solve each problem. Refer to the multiplication chart on page 36 if you need help.

A. $6\overline{)36}$ $7\overline{)42}$ $8\overline{)56}$ $5\overline{)45}$

B. $3\overline{)21}$ $9\overline{)63}$ $4\overline{)36}$ $6\overline{)54}$

C. $5\overline{)35}$ $3\overline{)27}$ $2\overline{)18}$ $7\overline{)49}$

D. $3\overline{)18}$ $6\overline{)24}$ $4\overline{)32}$ $9\overline{)54}$

E. $4\overline{)16}$ $2\overline{)14}$ $5\overline{)25}$ $8\overline{)64}$

F. $9\overline{)36}$ $4\overline{)24}$ $7\overline{)35}$ $5\overline{)30}$

G. $6\overline{)42}$ $2\overline{)16}$ $6\overline{)24}$ $5\overline{)40}$

H. $3\overline{)24}$ $7\overline{)21}$ $8\overline{)72}$ $9\overline{)81}$

Division with Remainders

Divisor → $3\overline{)19}$ ← **Dividend**

1. Think. How many times will 3 go into 19? 3 x 6 = 18.
2. Then, subtract. What is left is the **remainder**.

$$\begin{array}{r} 6\ r\ 1 \\ 3\overline{)19} \\ -18 \\ \hline 1 \end{array}$$

Study the example above. Then, solve each problem.

A. $2\overline{)15}$ $3\overline{)17}$ $4\overline{)19}$ $6\overline{)22}$

B. $4\overline{)25}$ $5\overline{)18}$ $7\overline{)23}$ $8\overline{)43}$

C. $9\overline{)70}$ $2\overline{)19}$ $4\overline{)21}$ $5\overline{)24}$

D. $7\overline{)30}$ $6\overline{)13}$ $8\overline{)25}$ $5\overline{)32}$

E. $4\overline{)17}$ $7\overline{)25}$ $9\overline{)42}$ $8\overline{)38}$

F. $5\overline{)19}$ $7\overline{)18}$ $8\overline{)17}$ $6\overline{)32}$

Division Practice

Study the examples on pages 43–45 and 47. Then, solve each problem.

A. $3\overline{)9}$ $4\overline{)12}$ $5\overline{)15}$ $7\overline{)28}$ $8\overline{)32}$

B. $9\overline{)72}$ $5\overline{)35}$ $6\overline{)42}$ $8\overline{)64}$ $7\overline{)49}$

C. $3\overline{)19}$ $4\overline{)15}$ $5\overline{)18}$ $7\overline{)22}$ $9\overline{)29}$

D. $6\overline{)37}$ $7\overline{)39}$ $8\overline{)25}$ $5\overline{)27}$ $4\overline{)34}$

E. $5\overline{)45}$ $2\overline{)12}$ $3\overline{)24}$ $6\overline{)36}$ $4\overline{)24}$

F. $7\overline{)50}$ $8\overline{)92}$ $6\overline{)20}$ $5\overline{)48}$ $3\overline{)16}$

Summer Bridge Math RB-904087

Connecting Operations

> Multiplication depends on equal groups. You can use multiplication basic facts to help you divide. The two are related, like families. They are called **fact families**. It looks like this:
>
>
>
> 4 groups of 3
> 4 x 3 = 12
>
> 12 divided into 4 equal groups
> 12 ÷ 4 = 3

Study the example above. Then, use the missing factor to help you find the quotient.

A.
2 x ☐ = 8

8 ÷ 2 = ☐

B.
3 x ☐ = 9

9 ÷ 3 = ☐

C.
4 x ☐ = 16

16 ÷ 4 = ☐

D.
8 x ☐ = 40

40 ÷ 8 = ☐

E.
5 x ☐ = 25

25 ÷ 5 = ☐

F.
6 x ☐ = 18

18 ÷ 6 = ☐

G.
4 x ☐ = 12

12 ÷ 4 = ☐

H.
7 x ☐ = 42

42 ÷ 7 = ☐

I.
3 x ☐ = 15

15 ÷ 3 = ☐

J.
9 x ☐ = 81

81 ÷ 9 = ☐

K.
2 x ☐ = 10

10 ÷ 2 = ☐

L.
2 x ☐ = 4

4 ÷ 2 = ☐

M.
5 x ☐ = 20

20 ÷ 5 = ☐

N.
3 x ☐ = 6

6 ÷ 3 = ☐

O.
6 x ☐ = 36

36 ÷ 6 = ☐

Summer Bridge Math RB-904087

Fact Families

A **fact family** is made up of three numbers that are related. The numbers can be used in a set of math problems. Just like addition and subtraction facts, multiplication and division facts are related.

$$\underline{\quad 2 \quad} \times \underline{\quad 3 \quad} = \underline{\quad 6 \quad}$$
$$\underline{\quad 3 \quad} \times \underline{\quad 2 \quad} = \underline{\quad 6 \quad}$$
$$\underline{\quad 6 \quad} \div \underline{\quad 3 \quad} = \underline{\quad 2 \quad}$$
$$\underline{\quad 6 \quad} \div \underline{\quad 2 \quad} = \underline{\quad 3 \quad}$$

Study the example above. Then, write two multiplication and two division equations for each fact family.

A.

_____ X _____ = _____
_____ X _____ = _____
_____ ÷ _____ = _____
_____ ÷ _____ = _____

B.

_____ X _____ = _____
_____ X _____ = _____
_____ ÷ _____ = _____
_____ ÷ _____ = _____

C.

_____ X _____ = _____
_____ X _____ = _____
_____ ÷ _____ = _____
_____ ÷ _____ = _____

D.

7
8 56

_____ X _____ = _____
_____ X _____ = _____
_____ ÷ _____ = _____
_____ ÷ _____ = _____

Summer Bridge Math RB-904087

Mixed Practice

Study the examples on pages 35 and 43–45. Then, solve each problem.

A.
$$\begin{array}{r} 6 \\ \times\ 8 \\ \hline \end{array} \qquad \begin{array}{r} 7 \\ \times\ 3 \\ \hline \end{array} \qquad \begin{array}{r} 8 \\ \times\ 2 \\ \hline \end{array} \qquad \begin{array}{r} 9 \\ \times\ 4 \\ \hline \end{array} \qquad \begin{array}{r} 2 \\ \times\ 7 \\ \hline \end{array}$$

B.
$$\begin{array}{r} 4 \\ \times\ 9 \\ \hline \end{array} \qquad \begin{array}{r} 3 \\ \times\ 8 \\ \hline \end{array} \qquad \begin{array}{r} 4 \\ \times\ 4 \\ \hline \end{array} \qquad \begin{array}{r} 6 \\ \times\ 2 \\ \hline \end{array} \qquad \begin{array}{r} 3 \\ \times\ 5 \\ \hline \end{array}$$

C.
$$\begin{array}{r} 8 \\ \times\ 8 \\ \hline \end{array} \qquad \begin{array}{r} 6 \\ \times\ 5 \\ \hline \end{array} \qquad \begin{array}{r} 2 \\ \times\ 3 \\ \hline \end{array} \qquad \begin{array}{r} 4 \\ \times\ 7 \\ \hline \end{array} \qquad \begin{array}{r} 2 \\ \times\ 9 \\ \hline \end{array}$$

D.
$$\begin{array}{r} 5 \\ \times\ 6 \\ \hline \end{array} \qquad \begin{array}{r} 8 \\ \times\ 7 \\ \hline \end{array} \qquad \begin{array}{r} 4 \\ \times\ 5 \\ \hline \end{array} \qquad \begin{array}{r} 7 \\ \times\ 7 \\ \hline \end{array} \qquad \begin{array}{r} 9 \\ \times\ 8 \\ \hline \end{array}$$

E. $9\overline{)81}$ $7\overline{)35}$ $4\overline{)32}$ $6\overline{)48}$

F. $5\overline{)45}$ $4\overline{)24}$ $9\overline{)63}$ $8\overline{)56}$

G. $9\overline{)72}$ $7\overline{)42}$ $6\overline{)18}$ $3\overline{)21}$

H. $8\overline{)40}$ $6\overline{)54}$ $8\overline{)64}$ $9\overline{)36}$

Summer Bridge Math RB-904087

Telling Time

8:00

The short hand is called the **hour hand**. It tells the hour. The long hand is the **minute hand**. It tells the minutes. On the left, the clock's hour hand is on the 8. The minute hand is on the 12. It shows 8 o'clock. On the right, the clock's minute hand is on the 6. It shows 8:30. We say this as "eight-thirty."

8:30

Study the examples above. Then, write the time shown on each clock.

A.

_____ : _____   _____ : _____   _____ : _____

B.

_____ : _____   _____ : _____   _____ : _____

Five-Minute Intervals

The minute hand takes 5 minutes to move from one number on the clock to the next. We count by fives as the minute hand moves to the next number. To read this clock, we say:

20 minutes past 3:00

3:20

40 minutes past 9:00

9:40

Study the examples above. Then, write each time two ways.

A. _____ minutes past _____ : _____

_____ : _____

B. _____ minutes past _____ : _____

_____ : _____

C. _____ minutes past _____ : _____

_____ : _____

D. _____ minutes past _____ : _____

_____ : _____

E. _____ minutes past _____ : _____

_____ : _____

F. _____ minutes past _____ : _____

_____ : _____

G. _____ minutes past _____ : _____

_____ : _____

H. _____ minutes past _____ : _____

_____ : _____

I. _____ minutes past _____ : _____

_____ : _____

J. _____ minutes past _____ : _____

_____ : _____

53

Drawing Hands on Clocks

Study the examples on pages 52 and 53. Then, draw the hands on each clock to show the time.

A.

8:35

B.

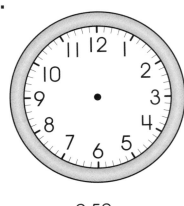

9:50

C.

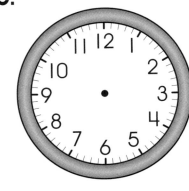

6:47

D.

12:23

E.

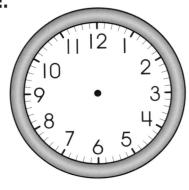

10:25

F.

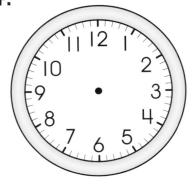

7:53

G.

11:08

H.

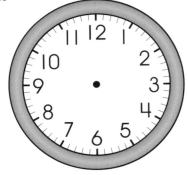

4:47

I.

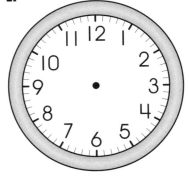

6:17

Introduction to Money

These are five commonly used **coins** in the United States.

50¢   25¢   10¢   5¢   1¢

The amount that coins are worth is called their **value**. You can find the total value of coins by adding one amount to another amount. This is called **counting on**.

50¢ ⟶ 75¢ ⟶ 85¢ ⟶ 90¢ ⟶ 95¢ ⟶ 96¢ ⟶ 97¢

Study the example above. Then, count on to find the total value.

A.

= ☐ ¢

B.

= ☐ ¢

C.

= ☐ ¢

D.

= ☐ ¢

E.

= ☐ ¢

F.

= ☐ ¢

G.

= ☐ ¢

H.

= ☐ ¢

Skip Counting Coins

It is easier to count coins if you **skip count** by the coin's value.

__10__¢ __20__¢ __30__¢ __35__¢ __40__¢ __45__¢ __50__¢ __55__¢   Total __55__¢

Study the example above and the coin values on page 55. Then, practice skip counting using the coins shown.

A.

____¢ ____¢ ____¢ ____¢ ____¢ ____¢ ____¢ ____¢   Total ____¢

B.

____¢ ____¢ ____¢ ____¢ ____¢ ____¢ ____¢ ____¢   Total ____¢

C.

____¢ ____¢ ____¢ ____¢ ____¢ ____¢ ____¢ ____¢   Total ____¢

D.

____¢ ____¢ ____¢ ____¢ ____¢ ____¢ ____¢ ____¢   Total ____¢

E.

____¢ ____¢ ____¢ ____¢ ____¢ ____¢ ____¢ ____¢   Total ____¢

F.

____¢ ____¢ ____¢ ____¢ ____¢ ____¢ ____¢ ____¢   Total ____¢

Counting Money

We write I dollar as $1.00. We say $1.35 as "one dollar and thirty-five cents."

$1.35

$1.00 = 100¢

$5.00

$10.00

$20.00

Study the money values above and on page 55. Then, count the money to find the total value.

A.

_____

B.

_____

C.

_____

D.

_____

E.

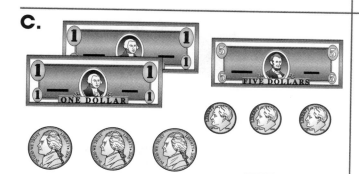

_____

F.

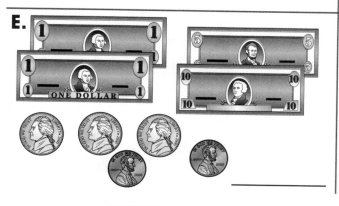 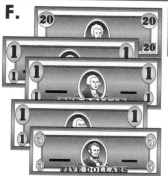 

_____

Summer Bridge Math RB-904087

Calculating Change

Sometimes when you pay for something, you get **change** back. You can figure your change using these steps:

1. Begin with the amount you paid the cashier.
2. Subtract the amount you owe from the amount you paid. Make sure to keep the **decimal points** lined up.
3. The difference is your change.

$$\begin{array}{r} {\scriptstyle 4\ \ 9\ 10} \\ \$\cancel{5}.\cancel{0}\cancel{0} \\ -\ 0.75 \\ \hline \$4.25 \end{array}$$

Line up the decimal points. ↑

Study the example above. Then, find the amount of change that will be given to the customer.

A. Paid $6.00 Owe − 2.10	**B.** Paid $20.00 Owe − 16.20	
C. Paid $8.00 Owe − 3.95	**D.** Paid $10.00 Owe − 4.60	
E. Paid $9.00 Owe − 8.50	**F.** Paid $5.00 Owe − 0.95	
G. Paid $16.00 Owe − 15.15	**H.** Paid $20.00 Owe − 5.00	
I. Paid $2.00 Owe − 1.19	**J.** Paid $4.00 Owe − 3.95	
K. Paid $10.00 Owe − 7.49	**L.** Paid $12.00 Owe − 11.23	

Summer Bridge Math RB-904087

Standard Measurement

inches = 1 inch	12 inches = 1 foot

Complete each sentence. Choose the measurement that makes the most sense.

A.	My Dad is _____ tall.	6 inches	6 feet
B.	My math book is _____ wide.	9 inches	9 feet
C.	My big toe is _____ long.	1 inch	1 foot
D.	My new baby sister is _____ long.	20 inches	20 feet

Measure the shape at the right with a ruler.

E. What is the length of the rectangle? _____ inches

F. What is the width of the rectangle? _____ inches

G. Add the measurements of the 4 sides of the rectangle to find its perimeter.

_____ inches + _____ inches + _____ inches + _____ inches = _____ inches

59
© Rainbow Bridge Publishing   **Summer Bridge Math** RB-904087

Comparing Linear Measurements

What would you use to measure the distance around your house? What would you use to find the distance to a nearby city? You would probably not use the same unit of measurement for both of these jobs. Compare the common units of measurement listed in the chart below.

Unit	To estimate, use:	Equal to:
centimeter (cm)	width of your finger	
meter (m)	width of a doorway	100 cm
kilometer (km)	distance you walk in 15 minutes	1000 m
inch (in.)	width of two fingers	
foot (ft.)	height of this paper	12 in.
yard (yd.)	length of a baseball bat	3 ft. or 36 in.
mile	distance you walk in 25 minutes	1,760 yd.

Use the table above to find the equivalent measurements.

A. 1000 m = _____ km   2 ft. = _____ in.   48 in. = _____ ft.

B. 1 ft. = _____ in.   3 ft. = _____ yd.   2 yd. = _____ ft.

C. 1 yd. = _____ in.   24 in. = _____ ft.   2000 m = _____ km

D. 2 m = _____ cm   4 km = _____ m   36 in. = _____ ft.

Compare using <, >, or =.

E. 1 ft. ( ) 1 yd.   1 ft. ( ) 1 in.

F. 4 yd. ( ) 1 mile   1 yd. ( ) 2 ft.

G. 4 in. ( ) 4 miles   24 in. ( ) 2 ft.

H. 1 ft. ( ) 12 in.   1 mile ( ) 1 km

Summer Bridge Math RB-904087   © Rainbow Bridge Publishing

Increments and Weight

Have you ever noticed all of the small lines along the top of a scale? They divide the scale into equal **increments**, or parts. Sometimes, the measurement you want is between two numbers. These measurements are marked with smaller lines. You must find the increment pattern of the smaller lines.

Count by ones.
Scale shows 44.

Count by twos.
Scale shows 36.

Count by fives.
Scale shows 45.

Study the examples above. Then, read each scale. Write the measurment. Circle the best unit of measurement by using the weight chart below.

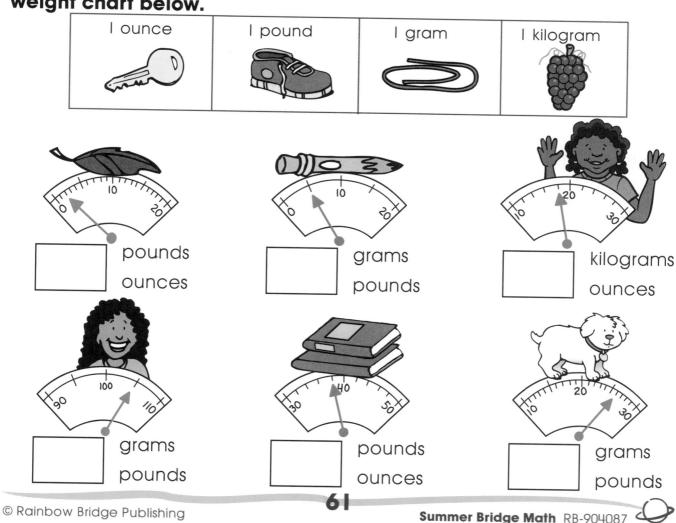

1 ounce	1 pound	1 gram	1 kilogram

pounds
ounces

grams
pounds

kilograms
ounces

grams
pounds

pounds
ounces

grams
pounds

Summer Bridge Math RB-904087

Capacity and Temperature

Capacity is the amount that a container can hold. Standard capacity can be measured in:

 I cup (c.)

 I pint (pt.) 2 c.

 I quart (qt.) 2 pt. 4 c.

 I gallon (gal.) 4 qt. 8 pt. 16 c.

Study the measurements above. Then, compare using <, >, or =.

A. 2 c. ◯ 2 gal.

2 pt. ◯ I qt.

5 c. ◯ I qt.

B. 3 pt. ◯ 2 qt.

3 qt. ◯ I gal.

I gal. ◯ 17 c.

C. I gal. ◯ 4 qt.

3 c. ◯ I pt.

2 qt. ◯ 4 pt.

Temperatures can be measured using either side of a thermometer. One side shows **Fahrenheit (°F)**, which is the standard unit of measure. The other side shows **Celsius (°C)**, which is the metric unit of measure. If the reading is below zero, write the temperature using a negative sign.
Example: −23°F

Write the temperature in °F and °C for each thermometer. Then, list two articles of clothing you would wear that day.

D. _____°F _____°C

I would wear

_____

_____

E. _____°F _____°C

I would wear

_____

_____

Introduction to Fractions

A **fraction** tells about equal parts of a whole. The top number is the **numerator**. It tells how many parts are shaded. The bottom number is the **denominator**. It tells how many parts in all.

Parts shaded ➞ $\dfrac{1}{6}$

Parts in all ➞

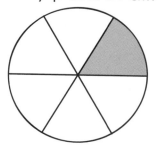

Study the example above. Then, write each fraction.

A.

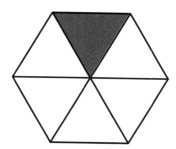

B.

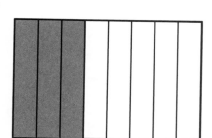

C.

D.

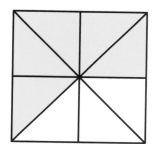

E.

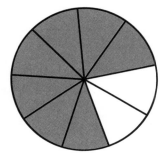

F.

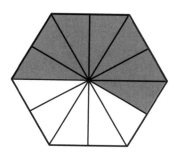

63

Equivalent Fractions

Equivalent fractions are fractions that are equal. To find equivalent fractions, multiply the numerator and the denominator of a fraction by the same number.

$$\frac{1 \times (2) = 2}{2 \times (2) = 4} \qquad \frac{1 \times (3) = 3}{2 \times (3) = 6}$$

Study the example above. Then, fill in the missing numerals to show equivalent fractions.

A. $\dfrac{1}{3} = \dfrac{\Box}{6} = \dfrac{\Box}{9} = \dfrac{4}{\Box} = \dfrac{5}{\Box}$

B. $\dfrac{1}{4} = \dfrac{\Box}{8} = \dfrac{\Box}{12} = \dfrac{4}{\Box} = \dfrac{\Box}{20}$

C. $\dfrac{2}{3} = \dfrac{\Box}{6} = \dfrac{6}{\Box} = \dfrac{\Box}{12} = \dfrac{10}{\Box}$

D. $\dfrac{3}{4} = \dfrac{6}{\Box} = \dfrac{9}{\Box} = \dfrac{\Box}{\Box} = \dfrac{\Box}{\Box}$

E. $\dfrac{4}{5} = \dfrac{\Box}{10} \qquad \dfrac{3}{7} = \dfrac{\Box}{21} \qquad \dfrac{4}{7} = \dfrac{16}{\Box} \qquad \dfrac{3}{4} = \dfrac{21}{\Box}$

F. $\dfrac{7}{8} = \dfrac{14}{\Box} \qquad \dfrac{5}{6} = \dfrac{\Box}{18} \qquad \dfrac{2}{7} = \dfrac{12}{\Box} \qquad \dfrac{2}{5} = \dfrac{\Box}{20}$

Summer Bridge Math RB-904087

Comparing Fractions

Fractions describe equal parts of a whole. They look like this:

 $= \dfrac{1}{2}$ ← part shaded
← total parts

$= \dfrac{6}{12}$ ← part shaded
← total parts

Larger numbers do not always mean larger fractions. We can compare fractions using <, >, and =.

 $\dfrac{1}{3}$ ⊙ $\dfrac{1}{6}$

Study the examples above. Then, write a fraction for each picture. Compare the two fractions using <, >, or = .

A.

B.

C.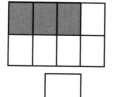

D.

E.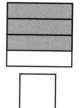

F.

65

Adding and Subtracting Fractions

The top and bottom numbers in a fraction have different meanings. They also have different names.

$\dfrac{3}{4}$ ← numerator
← denominator

To add or subtract fractions, the denominators must be the same. The denominator in the answer will also be the same. Add or subtract the numerators only.

$$\dfrac{1}{3} + \dfrac{1}{3} = \dfrac{2}{3}$$

2 ← added numerators, 1 + 1
3 ← denominator stays the same

Study the example above. Then, solve each problem.

A. $\dfrac{2}{4} + \dfrac{1}{4} = \dfrac{\Box}{\Box}$ $\dfrac{6}{8} - \dfrac{4}{8} = \dfrac{\Box}{\Box}$ $\dfrac{1}{5} + \dfrac{3}{5} = \dfrac{\Box}{\Box}$

B. $\dfrac{4}{10} + \dfrac{5}{10} = \dfrac{\Box}{\Box}$ $\dfrac{7}{8} - \dfrac{5}{8} = \dfrac{\Box}{\Box}$ $\dfrac{9}{10} - \dfrac{3}{10} = \dfrac{\Box}{\Box}$

C. $\dfrac{6}{9} + \dfrac{2}{9} = \dfrac{\Box}{\Box}$ $\dfrac{42}{100} + \dfrac{36}{100} = \dfrac{\Box}{\Box}$ $\dfrac{10}{12} - \dfrac{6}{12} = \dfrac{\Box}{\Box}$

Improper Fractions

When a fraction, such as $\frac{5}{3}$, has a numerator that is larger than the denominator, it is called an **improper fraction**. The fraction $\frac{3}{3}$ equals 1, so $\frac{5}{3}$ equals 1 and $\frac{2}{3}$. The answer $1\frac{2}{3}$ is called a **mixed number**.

To change an improper fraction to a mixed number, divide the numerator by the denominator and place any remainder as the numerator. $\frac{13}{3} = 13 \div 3 = 4$ with 1 remaining, or $4\frac{1}{3}$.

Study the examples above. Then, rewrite each fraction as a mixed number.

A. $\dfrac{14}{3} = $ _____ $\dfrac{12}{5} = $ _____ $\dfrac{17}{4} = $ _____ $\dfrac{13}{2} = $ _____

B. $\dfrac{12}{7} = $ _____ $\dfrac{18}{5} = $ _____ $\dfrac{27}{4} = $ _____ $\dfrac{23}{5} = $ _____

C. $\dfrac{11}{3} = $ _____ $\dfrac{15}{4} = $ _____ $\dfrac{24}{5} = $ _____ $\dfrac{19}{3} = $ _____

D. $\dfrac{38}{4} = $ _____ $\dfrac{66}{8} = $ _____ $\dfrac{44}{6} = $ _____ $\dfrac{84}{9} = $ _____

E. $\dfrac{18}{8} = $ _____ $\dfrac{26}{6} = $ _____ $\dfrac{39}{6} = $ _____ $\dfrac{42}{8} = $ _____

Sequencing Decimals

To sequence **decimals** with **whole numbers,** like 1, 2, and 3, write the whole numbers as decimals. **Example:** 1.0, 2.0, and 3.0. Then, compare the numbers as usual.

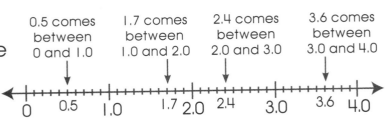

Study the example above. Then, write the missing numbers.

A.

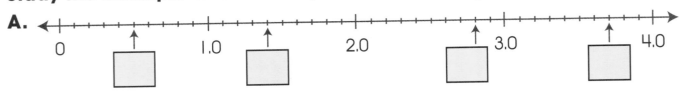

B.

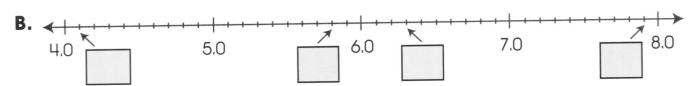

Write the numbers in order from least to greatest. Imagine a number line to help you.

C.

0.1	1.6
0.7	1.3

→

D.

2.4	1.9
0.8	0.3

→

E.

3.6	2.8
3.1	0.5

→

F.

2.6	2.1	2.8
1.4	0.9	

→

68

Using Decimals

Fractions that are **tenths** ($\frac{1}{10}$) or **hundredths** ($\frac{1}{100}$) are easy to write as decimals. Hint: When there are no whole numbers, put a zero in the ones place.

    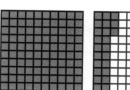

$\frac{4}{10}$ = four tenths
= 0.4

$1\frac{3}{10}$ = one and three tenths
= 1.3

$\frac{14}{100}$ = fourteen hundredths
= 0.14

$1\frac{23}{100}$ = one and twenty-three hundredths
= 1.23

Study the examples above. Then, write each fraction as a decimal number. Color the balloons with tenths blue. Color the balloons with hundredths green.

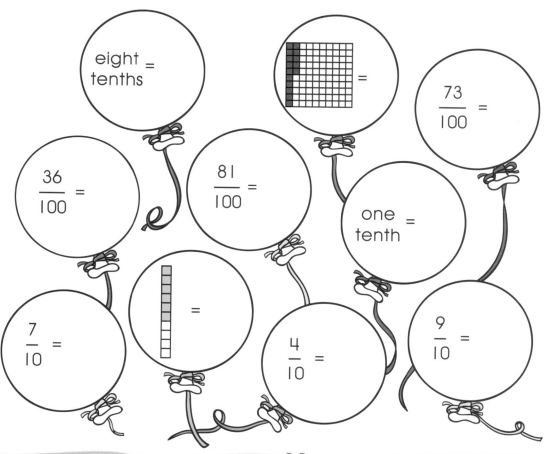

eight tenths =

 =

$\frac{73}{100}$ =

$\frac{36}{100}$ =

$\frac{81}{100}$ =

one tenth =

$\frac{7}{10}$ =

=

$\frac{4}{10}$ =

$\frac{9}{10}$ =

69

Adding and Subtracting Decimals

To add and subtract decimals, follow these steps:
1. Line up the decimal points.
2. Add or subtract beginning with the column farthest to the right. Regroup if needed.
3. Add or subtract the next column. Regroup if needed.
4. Continue to add or subtract each column, working to the left. Be sure to place the decimal point in your answer.

$$
\begin{array}{r} 3.\overset{5}{\cancel{6}}\overset{1}{6} \\ -\ 0.48 \\ \hline 3.18 \end{array}
\qquad
\begin{array}{r} \overset{1}{2}.4 \\ +\ 1.8 \\ \hline 4.2 \end{array}
$$

Study the examples above. Then, solve each problem.

A.
$$
\begin{array}{r} 2.6 \\ +\ 5.6 \\ \hline \end{array}
\qquad
\begin{array}{r} 6.7 \\ -\ 2.9 \\ \hline \end{array}
\qquad
\begin{array}{r} 3.52 \\ +\ 0.78 \\ \hline \end{array}
$$

B.
$$
\begin{array}{r} 9.59 \\ +\ 0.18 \\ \hline \end{array}
\qquad
\begin{array}{r} 7.34 \\ -\ 2.16 \\ \hline \end{array}
\qquad
\begin{array}{r} 1.8 \\ +\ 5.9 \\ \hline \end{array}
$$

C.
$$
\begin{array}{r} 8.09 \\ +\ 1.36 \\ \hline \end{array}
\qquad
\begin{array}{r} 7.3 \\ -\ 0.9 \\ \hline \end{array}
\qquad
\begin{array}{r} 6.3 \\ -\ 4.8 \\ \hline \end{array}
$$

D.
$$
\begin{array}{r} 6.03 \\ +\ 1.81 \\ \hline \end{array}
\qquad
\begin{array}{r} 2.38 \\ -\ 0.16 \\ \hline \end{array}
\qquad
\begin{array}{r} 4.99 \\ -\ 2.83 \\ \hline \end{array}
\qquad
\begin{array}{r} 9.4 \\ -\ 0.7 \\ \hline \end{array}
\qquad
\begin{array}{r} 3.7 \\ +\ 3.9 \\ \hline \end{array}
$$

Summer Bridge Math RB-904087

Tenths

Study the examples on page 68 and 69. Then, write each fraction as a decimal.

A. $\dfrac{3}{10}$ = ___ $\dfrac{5}{10}$ = ___ $\dfrac{9}{10}$ = ___ $\dfrac{2}{10}$ = ___

B. $\dfrac{8}{10}$ = ___ $\dfrac{4}{10}$ = ___ $\dfrac{7}{10}$ = ___ $\dfrac{6}{10}$ = ___

Write each decimal as a fraction.

C.   0.6 = ___   0.4 = ___   0.7 = ___   0.8 = ___

D.   0.3 = ___   0.5 = ___   0.2 = ___   0.9 = ___

Study the examples on pages 67 and 69. Then, write the improper fraction, the mixed number, and the decimal for each problem.

E.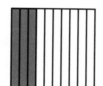

fractions: ___ or 1 ___

decimal: ___

F.

fractions: ___ or 1 ___

decimal: ___

G.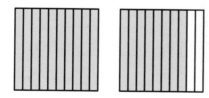

fractions: ___ or 1 ___

decimal: ___

H.

fractions: ___ or ___

decimal: ___

Summer Bridge Math RB-904087

Tenths Practice

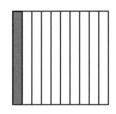

Example:

_____ tenth

$\dfrac{1}{10}$ _____ fraction

_____ decimal
(1, 1/10, 0.1)

Study the examples above and on page 69. Then, write the tenths, the fraction, and the decimal for each problem.

A.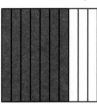

_____ tenths

_____ fraction

_____ decimal

B.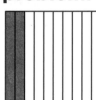

_____ tenths

_____ fraction

_____ decimal

C.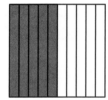

_____ tenths

_____ fraction

_____ decimal

D.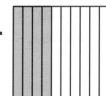

_____ tenths

_____ fraction

_____ decimal

E.

_____ tenths

_____ fraction

_____ decimal

F.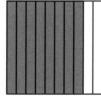

_____ tenths

_____ fraction

_____ decimal

G.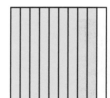

_____ tenths

_____ fraction

_____ decimal

H.

_____ tenths

_____ fraction

_____ decimal

I. Illustrate $\dfrac{10}{10}$ or I whole.

_____ tenths

_____ fraction

_____ decimal

Place Value Practice

Study the examples below. Then, write how many ones, tenths, and hundredths each decimal contains.

	ones	tenths	hundredths
0.6	0	6	0
A. 1.07			
B. 5.60			
C. 3.91			
D. 16.06			
E. 0.13			
F. 7.93			

	ones	tenths	hundredths
4.3	4	3	0
G. 3.01			
H. 1.25			
I. 4.11			
J. 2.53			
K. 9.1			
L. 8.84			

Study the examples below and on page 69. Then, solve each problem. Shade in the boxes to show your answer.

0.06 + 0.03 = _____0.09_____

M.   1.46 + 0.34 = _____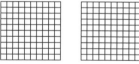

N.   1.5 + 1.7 = _____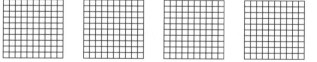

O.   2.4 + 1.8 = _____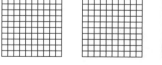

P.   0.37 + 2.70 = _____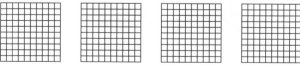

Q.   2.55 + 1.68 = _____

73

Predicting Patterns

By studying a given picture, you can determine its **pattern** and predict what will come next.

Study the example above. Then, continue each pattern with three more pictures. Use another sheet of paper if you need more room.

A.

B.

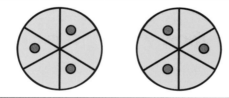

C.

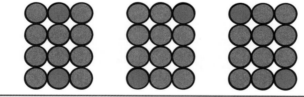

D.

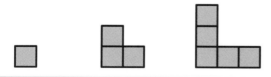

E.

F.

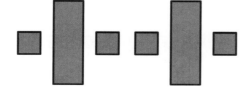

Number Patterns

Follow the directions.

A. Skip count by 3. Color all of those numbers red. What pattern do you see?

1	2	3	4	5	6	7	8	9	10
11	12	13	14	15	16	17	18	19	20
21	22	23	24	25	26	27	28	29	30
31	32	33	34	35	36	37	38	39	40
41	42	43	44	45	46	47	48	49	50
51	52	53	54	55	56	57	58	59	60
61	62	63	64	65	66	67	68	69	70
71	72	73	74	75	76	77	78	79	80
81	82	83	84	85	86	87	88	89	90
91	92	93	94	95	96	97	98	99	100

B. Skip count by 4. Color all of those numbers blue. What pattern do you see?

1	2	3	4	5	6	7	8	9	10
11	12	13	14	15	16	17	18	19	20
21	22	23	24	25	26	27	28	29	30
31	32	33	34	35	36	37	38	39	40
41	42	43	44	45	46	47	48	49	50
51	52	53	54	55	56	57	58	59	60
61	62	63	64	65	66	67	68	69	70
71	72	73	74	75	76	77	78	79	80
81	82	83	84	85	86	87	88	89	90
91	92	93	94	95	96	97	98	99	100

C. Skip count by 6. Color all of those numbers green. What pattern do you see?

1	2	3	4	5	6	7	8	9	10
11	12	13	14	15	16	17	18	19	20
21	22	23	24	25	26	27	28	29	30
31	32	33	34	35	36	37	38	39	40
41	42	43	44	45	46	47	48	49	50
51	52	53	54	55	56	57	58	59	60
61	62	63	64	65	66	67	68	69	70
71	72	73	74	75	76	77	78	79	80
81	82	83	84	85	86	87	88	89	90
91	92	93	94	95	96	97	98	99	100

D. Skip count by 11. Color all of those numbers yellow. What pattern do you see?

1	2	3	4	5	6	7	8	9	10
11	12	13	14	15	16	17	18	19	20
21	22	23	24	25	26	27	28	29	30
31	32	33	34	35	36	37	38	39	40
41	42	43	44	45	46	47	48	49	50
51	52	53	54	55	56	57	58	59	60
61	62	63	64	65	66	67	68	69	70
71	72	73	74	75	76	77	78	79	80
81	82	83	84	85	86	87	88	89	90
91	92	93	94	95	96	97	98	99	100

Patterns and Functions

Finding patterns is helpful in solving problems. Look at the **number pattern** here. The left column includes the numbers that plug into the brackets [ ] in the "Rule." The right column shows the answers. **Example:** Place 2 (the first number in the left column) in the rule. Then, solve the equation.

[2] x 3 = 6 and 6 + 2 = 8

Rule: [ ] x 3 + 2	
2	8
3	11
4	14
5	17
6	20
7	23
8	26

Study the example above. Then, look at the pattern. Fill in the chart.

A.

Rule: [ ] x 2 + 1	
2	5
3	7
4	9
5	11
6	
7	
8	

B.

Rule: [ ] x 3 – 2	
2	4
3	7
4	10
5	
6	
7	
8	

C.

Rule: [ ] x 5 + 1	
2	11
3	16
4	21
5	
6	
7	
8	

D.

Rule: [ ] x 4 – 6	
2	2
3	6
4	10
5	
6	
7	
8	

E. What is the rule?

Rule: [ ] x –	
2	0
3	3
4	6
5	9
6	12
7	15
8	18

Summer Bridge Math RB-904087

Shapes

> **Parallel lines** run side by side and never cross.
>
> A **quadrilateral** is any shape with four sides.

Study the shapes. Then, answer each question.

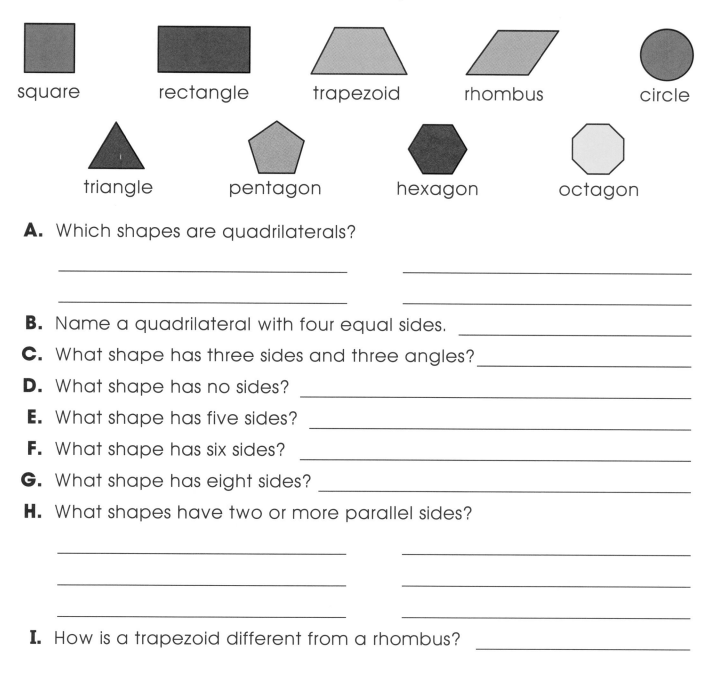

square   rectangle   trapezoid   rhombus   circle

triangle   pentagon   hexagon   octagon

A. Which shapes are quadrilaterals?

_____   _____

_____   _____

B. Name a quadrilateral with four equal sides. _____

C. What shape has three sides and three angles? _____

D. What shape has no sides? _____

E. What shape has five sides? _____

F. What shape has six sides? _____

G. What shape has eight sides? _____

H. What shapes have two or more parallel sides?

_____   _____

_____   _____

_____   _____

I. How is a trapezoid different from a rhombus? _____

_____

Summer Bridge Math RB-904087

Spatial Figures

Spatial figures are solids that take up space. The flat side of a figure is called a **face**.

cube (6 faces) sphere rectangular prism (6 faces) cone (1 face) pyramid (5 faces) cylinder (2 faces)

Study the figures above. Then, name the spatial figure that each object looks like. Write the number of faces.

A.

_____

_____ # of faces

B.

_____

_____ # of faces

C.

_____

_____ # of faces

D.

_____

_____ # of faces

E.

_____

_____ # of faces

F.

_____

_____ # of faces

G.

_____

_____ # of faces

H.

_____

_____ # of faces

I.

_____

_____ # of faces

J.

_____

_____ # of faces

K.

_____

_____ # of faces

Lines of Symmetry

A **line of symmetry** is a line that divides a figure into two identical parts. These are lines of symmetry:

 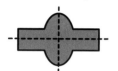

Study the examples above. Then, draw 1 line of symmetry for each object.

Draw two lines of symmetry for each figure.

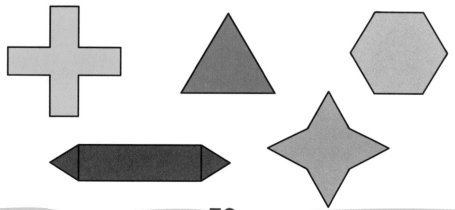

Summer Bridge Math RB-904087

Perimeter

> The **perimeter (P)** of a figure is the distance around that figure. The perimeter is measured in units, which may be inches, centimeters, miles, or any other unit of measuring length. To find the perimeter, add all of the sides together.

Find the perimeter of each figure. Label your answer in the units shown.

A.

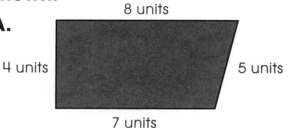

8 units
4 units
5 units
7 units

P = _____

B.

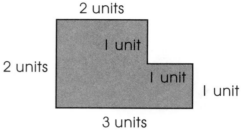

2 units
1 unit
2 units
1 unit
1 unit
3 units

P = _____

C.

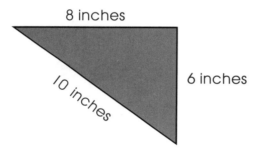

8 inches
10 inches
6 inches

P = _____

D.

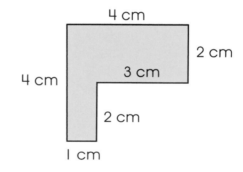

4 cm
2 cm
3 cm
4 cm
2 cm
1 cm

P = _____

E.

7 miles
7 miles
7 miles

P = _____

F.

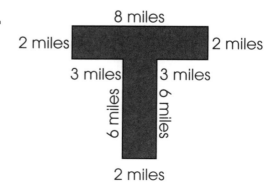

8 miles
2 miles
2 miles
3 miles
3 miles
6 miles
6 miles
2 miles

P = _____

Summer Bridge Math RB-904087

Exploring Probability

Probability is the chance of something happening. Imagine that you have 6 red apples and 3 green apples. Close your eyes and choose an apple. The probability is higher that you will choose a red apple rather than a green apple. To have equal chances, each choice must have an equal amount.

Look at the spinners below. Then, answer each question.

Spinner A

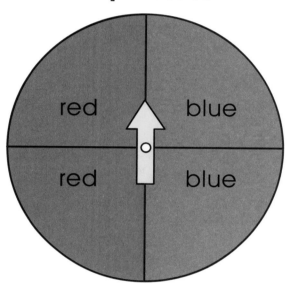

Spinner B

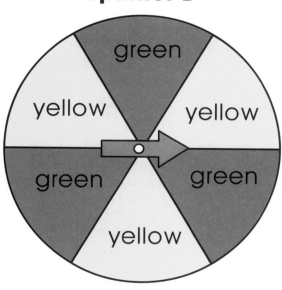

A. On Spinner A, would you have more chances of spinning red or blue, or would your chances be equal? _____

B. On Spinner B, would you have more chances of spinning yellow or green, or would your chances be equal? _____

C. What are the chances of spinning red on Spinner B? _____

D. On Spinner A, you have a 2 out of 4 chance of spinning either red or blue. On Spinner B, what chance out of 6 do you have of spinning green? _____

E. On Spinner B, what chance out of 6 do you have of spinning yellow?

_____

Summer Bridge Math RB-904087

Reading a Chart

> The **title** of a chart tells you what the chart is about.

Study the chart. Then, answer each question.

Wednesday Night Television Schedule

	7:00	7:30	8:00	8:30	9:00	9:30	10:00	10:30
2	Million Dollar Game Show	Jump Start		News Magazine			News	
4	Lucky Guess	You Should Know	Wednesday Night at the Movies *Friends Forever*				News	
5	Best Friends	Sarah's Secret	Where They Are	Time to Hope	Tom's Talk Show		News	
7	Freakin' Out	Lost Alone	Last One Standing	Sports Tonight			News	
11	Your Health	Eating Right	Nutrition News		Cooking with Kate		Home Decorating	Shopping Show
24	Silly Rabbit	Clyde the Clown	Your Lucky Day	Slime & Rhyme	Cartoon Alley		Fun Times	Make Me Laugh

A. What information does this chart give? _____

_____

B. What time is *Slime & Rhyme* on Channel 24? _____

C. What channel is *Tom's Talk Show* on at 9:00? _____

D. What show is on Channel 11 at 7:30? _____

E. How long is the Wednesday night movie on Channel 4? _____

F. On how many channels can you watch news at 10:00? _____

G. How many shows start at 8:00? _____

H. What would you choose to watch at 9:00? _____

Interpreting Graphs and Grids

The **line graph** below shows points of information. Lines are then drawn between the **points** to make an easy comparison. This line graph shows the temperature change throughout one week.

Study the graph below. Then, answer each question.

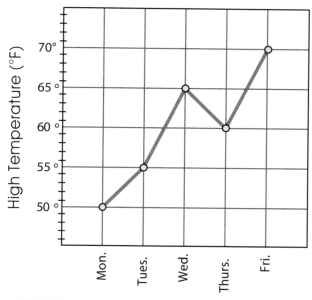

A. What was the difference in temperature from Wednesday to Friday? _____

B. How many degrees did the temperature drop from Wednesday to Thursday? _____

C. What was the lowest temperature reading? _____ °F

D. What was the difference in temperature from Monday to Thursday? _____

This is a **coordinate grid**. It is used to show the location of something. The numbers along the bottom and side describe the location using an ordered pair. The first number is from the bottom of the grid, and the second number is from the side of the grid. For example, the raindrop is found at (6, 3). Can you find it?

Draw the symbols found at:

E. 2,3 _____

F. 4,1 _____

G. 3,5 _____

H. Write each ordered pair.

 _____    _____

83

Addition and Subtraction

> **Problem solving** means using the information from a story to solve a math problem.
>
> **Example:** John ate 12 grapes. Then, he ate 10 more. How many grapes did he eat in all? 12 + 10 = 22, so John ate 22 grapes.

Study the example above. Then, solve each problem.

A. Anthony made 9 clay pots. He broke 4 of the pots. How many pots does he have left?

B. Keenan had 17 boxes of candy to sell. He sold 2 boxes to his grandma. His dad sold 9 boxes to people at work. How many more boxes did Keenan have to sell?

C. Min collects trading cards. She wants to collect all 15 cards in a series. She already has 8 of the cards. How many more cards does Min need?

D. Trina had 7 fish in her aquarium. She bought 4 more fish. How many fish does she have altogether?

E. Nina got 16 pieces of candy from the piñata. She ate 7 pieces. How many does she have left?

F. Bradley read 5 books the first month of summer break and 8 books the second month. How many books did he read in all?

Three-Digit Addition and Subtraction

Read the word problems carefully. Look for the key words to help you know whether to add or subtract to find the answer.

Add	Subtract
how many in all	how many more
how many together	how many left

Study the key words above and the example on page 84. Then, solve each problem.

A. Anthony had 348 pennies. His brother had 239. How many more pennies did Anthony have than his brother?

B. Celeste collected 479 aluminum cans. Nicole collected 742 cans. How many cans did the girls collect altogether?

C. The electronics store had 371 televisions in stock. They sold 138 on the weekend. How many televisions do they have left?

D. My big brother Matt weighs 189 pounds. His friend weighs 202 pounds. How much less does Matt weigh than his friend?

E. The school library has 879 nonfiction books and 932 fiction books. How many books does the library have altogether?

F. The girls earned 487 points for selling cookies. The boys earned 399 points. How many more points did the girls earn than the boys?

Multiplication

Some word problems can be answered using multiplication. They ask you to find a total number, similar to addition. The difference is that these stories involve equal sets.

Example: Matthew ordered 3 ice cream cones. Each cone had 2 scoops. How many scoops of ice cream did Matthew order?

$$3 \times 2 = 6$$

number of sets   number in each set   total scoops ordered

Study the example above. Then, solve each problem. Show your work.

A. Tina rode her bike 17 miles each day for 6 days. How many miles did Tina ride?

B. Jack read 7 books. Each book had 48 pages. How many pages did Jack read?

C. Marissa has 5 trading card books. Each book has 50 cards in it. How many trading cards does Marissa have?

D. Juan put his stamp collection into 4 boxes. He put 73 stamps in each box. How many stamps does he have?

Summer Bridge Math RB-904087   © Rainbow Bridge Publishing

Study the examples on pages 84 and 86. Then, solve each problem.

A. Bev's 3 guinea pigs ate 24 seeds each. How many seeds did the guinea pigs eat?

B. We found 6 spider webs. Each web had trapped 17 bugs. How many bugs were trapped?

C. A ticket to the game costs $26.00. Amy has $18.00. How much more does Amy need to buy a ticket?

D. Haley has 52 dimes in her bank. She has 39 nickels. How many coins does she have?

E. We passed 8 trucks on the highway. Each truck honked 4 times. How many honks did the trucks make in all?

F. Jon is making lemonade for 16 people. Each glass needs 3 spoons of powdered mix. How many spoons of powdered mix will Jon use?

Division

Other story problems can be answered using division. They ask you to find missing parts or make smaller groups. They also involve making equal sets.

Example: Yasmine had 9 hair ribbons. She split them evenly between 3 friends. How many ribbons did each friend get?

$$9 \div 3 = 3$$

total ribbons	number of groups	ribbons each

Study the example above. Then, solve each problem. Show your work.

A. The Millers have 6 children. When they come to the pool, they bring 36 toys to share equally among the children. How many toys does each child get?

B. Mrs. Weitz passed out 24 papers equally to 8 students. How many papers did each student get?

C. Tara and Sira share 12 cookies evenly. How many cookies does each girl get?

D. There are 88 total horse legs in the pasture. How many horses are there?

Division with Remainders

Sometimes, objects do not divide evenly into groups. There will be objects left over.

Example: There are 11 cookies. There are 3 children. How many cookies will each child get? How many cookies will be left over?

Each child gets 3 cookies. There are 2 cookies left over.

Study the example above. Then, solve each problem.

A. There are 14 pieces of paper. Miss Scriber places them in 3 equal stacks.

How many papers are in each stack? _____

How many papers are left over?

_____

B. Mark has 15 books. He put them on 2 shelves, with the same number of books on each shelf.

How many books are on each shelf? _____

How many books are left over?

_____

C. Alex has 11 apples. He needs 5 apples to make a pie. How many pies can he make?

_____

How many apples are left over?

_____

D. Jenny has 19 walnuts. She wants to divide them evenly between 3 bags.

How many walnuts will be in each bag? _____

How many walnuts are left over? _____

Time

A.M. refers to the morning time from 12:00 midnight until 12:00 noon. **P.M.** refers to the afternoon and evening time from 12:00 noon until 12:00 midnight. There are 60 minutes in one hour.

Solve each problem. Refer to the clock above if you need help.

A. Isabella wants to watch a show at 8:00 P.M. It is 7:23 P.M. How many more minutes is it until the show starts?

B. Cade's favorite show starts at 7:30 P.M. It is 90 minutes long. What time will the show end?

C. Taylor's favorite show started at 4:30 P.M. It is 30 minutes long. It is 4:53 P.M. right now. How many more minutes is the show on?

D. Melissa watched a movie that started at 7:00 P.M. It lasted 1 hour and 47 minutes. What time did the movie end?

E. Jonathan started watching a show at 4:16 P.M. He turned the television off at 5:37 P.M. How long did he watch television?

F. Chelsea watched 2 30-minute shows on Monday, 1 30-minute show on Wednesday, and 3 30-minute shows on Friday. How many hours of television did she watch that week?

Money

> Mike wants to buy a game that costs $23.00. He has saved $17.00. How much more does he need to save?
>
> Subtract $17.00 from $23.00 to find out how much more. Mike needs to save $6.00 more.
>
> $$\begin{array}{r} \$\cancel{2}3.00 \\ -\ \$17.00 \\ \hline \$\ \ 6.00 \end{array}$$

Study the example above. Then, solve each problem.

A. Gina had $17.22. She earned $5.00 more for helping her mother. How much money does Gina have now?

B. Matt had $18.77. He wanted to buy a CD for $14.50. How much would he have left if he bought the CD?

C. Josh got $3.50 from his mother, $4.00 from his father, and $10.00 from his grandparents. How much money did Josh get?

D. Len had $53.00. He was trying to earn enough money for a bike that cost $87.00. How much more money does he need?

E. Dan earned $20.00 for mowing the neighbor's yard. He already had $12.00. How much money does he have now?

F. Emma wanted to buy a science kit that cost $18.00. She only had $6.00. How much more money does she need?

Problem Solving Using Charts

Sometimes a story problem can be answered by writing the information in a chart.

Example: By the end of 1 week, the grass in Mr. Johnson's yard had grown to 3 inches. After 2 weeks, the grass was 6 inches high. If the pattern continues, how tall will Mr. Johnson's grass be after 6 weeks? Follow these steps:

1. Fill in the information from the story.
2. Figure out the pattern.
3. Complete the chart using the pattern.

Week #	1	2	3	4	5	6
Inches	3	6	9	12	15	18

Mr. Johnson's grass will be 18 inches tall after 6 weeks.

Study the example above. Then, complete each chart to solve the problem. Circle your answer in the chart.

A. Sparky likes to run around the house. It takes him 4 minutes to make it around 2 times. How long will it take Sparky to run around 10 times?

# of times										
# of minutes										

B. Patsy spends 3 hours every 2 days practicing her flute. After 4 days she has spent 6 hours practicing. How many hours will she practice in 12 days?

# of days										
# of hours										

Summer Bridge Math RB-904087

Answer Key

Page 7: ON HIS FEET!

Page 8: A. 6,911; **B.** 4,073;
C. 9,207; **D.** 839; **E.** 9,601; **F.** 8,390;
G. 417; **H.** 5,082; **I.** 470; **J.** 3,512;
K. 6,914; **L.** 4,413

Page 9: A. three hundred forty-
seven; **B.** two hundred seventy-
nine; **C.** nine hundred sixty;
D. seven hundred nineteen;
E. eight hundred one; **F.** five
hundred ninety; **G.** one hundred
thirty-five; **H.** five hundred nine;
I. six hundred eighty; **J.** nine
hundred ninety-nine; **K.** 313;
L. 809; **M.** 426; **N.** 211; **O.** 751;
P. 105; **Q.** 532; **R.** 944

Page 10: A. 5th, 6th, 7th, 8th, 9th,
10th; **B.** 21st, 22nd, 23rd, 24th,
26th, 27th; **C.** 80th, 81st, 82nd,
84th, 85th, 86th, 87th; **D.** 7; **E.** 5;
F. 12th

Page 11: A. 1, 3, 4, 5; 1,345; **B.** 2,
1, 6, 1; 2,161; **C.** 1, 0, 3, 0; 1,030;
D. 3, 1, 0, 0; 3,100; **E.** 2, 4, 4, 0;
2,440; **F.** 1, 2, 1, 3; 1,213

Page 12: A. 0, 5, 7, 3, 9; **B.** 1, 4, 6,
5, 0; **C.** 2, 7, 3, 8, 1; **D.** 4, 0, 7, 3,
6; **E.** 9, 1, 4, 7, 5; **F.** 5, 5, 8, 3, 7;
G. 8, 6, 9, 0, 2; **H.** 0, 4, 5, 6, 0;
I. 3, 1, 0, 4, 8; **J.** 1, 1, 1, 1, 1; **K.** 7,
9, 2, 7, 7; **L.** 6, 8, 5, 9, 3; **M.** 9, 9, 9,
9, 9; **N.** 4, 8, 3, 0, 5; **O.** hundreds,
hundreds; **P.** thousands, ten
thousands; **Q.** ten thousands,
tens; **R.** tens, ten thousands;
S. hundreds, thousands;
T. ones, tens; **U.** tens, ones;
V. ten thousands, ten thousands;
W. thousands, hundreds

Page 13: A. 9,000 + 500 + 10 + 6;
B. 2,000 + 300 + 50 + 8; **C.** 1,000 +
400 + 0 + 7; **D.** 0 + 900 + 20 + 1;
E. 7,000 + 800 + 0 + 0; **F.** 3,000 +
200 + 60 + 4; **G.** 5,000 + 100 + 80
+ 2; **H.** 0 + 600 + 10 + 4; **I.** 4,000 +
0 + 70 + 3; **J.** 9,000 + 500 + 30 + 0

Page 14: A. 1,533; **B.** 5,947;
C. 3,755; **D.** 7,479; **E.** 9,021;
F. 3,102; **G.** 3,506; **H.** 6,098;
I. 3,609; **J.** 1,698; **K.** 3,000 + 400 +
50 + 6; **L.** 7,000 + 300 + 20 + 4;
M. 9,000 + 100 + 50 + 2; **N.** 3,000 +
500 + 60 + 9; **O.** 2,000 + 400 + 30
+ 1; **P.** 4,000 + 20 + 2

Page 15: A. >; **B.** >; **C.** <; **D.** =;
E. <; **F.** >; **G.** <; **H.** <; **I.** =; **J.** <

Page 16: A. 149; **B.** 566; **C.** 430;
D. 390; **E.** 804; **F.** 981; **G.** 709;
H. 871; **I.** 990; **J.** 805; **K.** <, >;
L. <, >; **M.** <, <; **N.** >, <; **O.** >, <;
P. >, <; **Q.** >, <; **R.** >, <; **S.** <, <

Page 17: From left to right and
top to bottom: 100, 600, 300, 700,
900, 700, 500, 900

Page 18: A. 0, 4, 8, 12; **B.** 0, 6, 12;
C. 33, 36, 39, 42, 45; **D.** 62, 64, 66,
68, 70, 72, 74; **E.** 84, 88, 92, 96

Page 19: A. 65, 89, 78, 58, 85, 69;
B. 99, 93, 97, 99, 59, 89; **C.** 89, 96,
78, 79, 59, 59; **D.** 87, 99, 96, 89, 87,
71; **E.** 88, 85, 67, 78, 79, 86; **F.** 86,
79, 49, 99, 85, 74

Page 20: A. 51, 92, 81, 86, 64, 90;
B. 94, 130, 92, 92, 103, 75; **C.** 92,
111, 70, 114, 130, 140; **D.** 81, 83,
83, 61, 46, 86; **E.** 70, 62, 96, 90,
81, 76

Page 21: A. 885, 778, 988, 998,
527; **B.** 594, 986, 969, 789, 919;
C. 788, 985, 867, 877, 798; **D.** 786,
786, 879, 769, 888; **E.** 985, 678,
899, 957, 898; **F.** 956, 699, 969,
889, 859

Page 22: A. 451, 702, 816, 1,192,
830; **B.** 823, 851; 1,044; 1,013; 605;
C. 900, 813; 1,011; 1,177; 1,021;
D. 613, 821, 862, 750, 929;
E. 1,180; 1,405; 872, 894, 831;
F. 1,174; 974, 611, 794, 890

Page 23: A. 8,500; 6,712; 9,809;
9,080; 4,401; **B.** 6,308; 13,046;
8,180; 11,055; 9,742; **C.** 8,066;
11,195; 10,191; 9,809; 11,207;
D. 11,906; 7,600; 7,424; 11,039;
10,889; **E.** 5,008; 10,087; 6,041;
11,817; 11,817; **F.** 12,570; 7,715;
5,026; 6,102; 12,079

Page 24: A. 6, 7, 9, 10, 11, 11, 12;
B. 12, 10, 13, 14, 7, 10, 12; **C.** 13,
13, 11, 15, 17, 14, 18; **D.** 13, 15, 15,
18, 18, 18, 13; **E.** 16, 17, 17, 18, 18,
13, 18

Page 25: A. $11.37, $12.23;
B. $13.50, $16.53, $10.58;
C. $13.34, $18.08, $19.04;
D. $6.63, $12.70; The left castle is
located in the richest kingdom.

Page 26: A. 54, 40, 22, 65, 61, 15;
B. 26, 20, 24, 23, 51, 50; **C.** 32, 23,
4, 60, 24, 24; **D.** 22, 10, 40, 15, 26,
16; **E.** 72, 41, 50, 34, 41, 63

Page 27: A. 19, 79, 19, 26, 16, 49;
B. 19, 58, 14, 59, 28, 32; **C.** 28, 68,
36, 39, 14, 47; **D.** 25, 39, 59, 38, 48,
24; **E.** 38, 29, 49, 8, 58, 19

Page 28: A. 431, 213, 225, 236,
223; **B.** 553, 322, 812, 121, 205;
C. 63, 137, 462, 414, 142; **D.** 633,
342, 704, 312, 148; **E.** 220, 414,
260, 316, 541

Page 29: A. 699, 269, 469, 429,
257; **B.** 187, 292, 739, 289, 228;
C. 424, 338, 429, 449, 608; **D.** 584,
193, 691, 84, 470

Summer Bridge Math RB-904087

Answer Key

Page 30: A. 4,406; 1,296; 2,067; 2,947; 2,087; **B.** 4,728; 6,035; 3,760; 5,965; 1,082; **C.** 3,559; 5,032; 4,802; 2,058; 2,758; **D.** 909; 4,063; 1,879; 6,077; 7,367; **E.** 3,696; 4,086; 1,274; 4,663; 4,977

Page 31: A. 2,338; 3,729; 1,589; 3,820; **B.** 8,858; 2,612; 8,768; 485; **C.** 3,805; 7,388; 5,321; 458; **D.** 774; 2,479

Page 32: A. 58, 66, 28, 71, 92; **B.** 24, 59, 19, 81, 32; **C.** 60, 142, 12, 57, 92; **D.** 33, 85, 18, 87, 61; **E.** 39, 47, 19, 92, 89; **F.** 113, 74, 19, 82, 16

Page 33: A. 1,025; 307; 1,226; 1,012; 462; **B.** 732; 921; 118; 1,119; 349; **C.** 198; 822; 438; 1,381; 463; **D.** 823; 652; 507; 920; 508; **E.** 426; 459; 1,082; 1,024; 865; **F.** 1,234; 394; 831; 904; 928

Page 34: clockwise from the top: 240, 600, 350, 342, 999, 785

Page 35: A. 5 + 5 + 5 = 15, 3 x 5 = 15; **B.** 3 + 3 = 6, 2 x 3 = 6; **C.** 2 + 2 + 2 + 2 = 8, 4 x 2 = 8; **D.** 4 + 4 = 8, 2 x 4 = 8; **E.** 3 + 3 + 3 = 9, 3 x 3 = 9; **F.** 4 + 4 + 4 = 12, 3 x 4 = 12; **G.** 2 + 2 + 2 = 6, 3 x 2 = 6; **H.** 5 + 5 = 10, 2 x 5 = 10

Page 36: Row 1: 2, 3, 4, 5, 6, 7, 8, 9; **Row 2:** 2, 4, 6, 8, 10, 12, 14, 16, 18; **Row 3:** 3, 6, 9, 12, 15, 18, 21, 24, 27; **Row 4:** 4, 8, 12, 16, 20, 24, 28, 32, 36; **Row 5:** 5, 10, 15, 20, 25, 30, 35, 40, 45; **Row 6:** 6, 12, 18, 24, 30, 36, 42, 48, 54; **Row 7:** 7, 14, 21, 28, 35, 42, 49, 56, 63; **Row 8:** 8, 16, 24, 32, 40, 48, 56, 64, 72; **Row 9:** 9, 18, 27, 36, 45, 54, 63, 72, 81; **A.** the number; **B.** They are all even numbers.; **C.** They end in 0 or 5.; **D.** 9; **E.** 12

Page 37: 1st riddle: YOUR RIGHT ELBOW; **2nd riddle:** BECAUSE FISH HAVE THEIR OWN SCALES

Page 38: A. 4, 6, 15, 6, 12; **B.** 16, 10, 12, 8, 2; **C.** 14, 18, 18, 16, 20; **D.** 27, 30, 24, 21, 24; **E.** 16, 30, 40, 63, 64; **F.** 20, 72, 42, 35, 32; **G.** 36, 28, 56, 81, 36; **H.** 20, 25, 45, 48, 28

Page 39: A. 48, 22, 26, 39; **B.** 33, 28, 36, 44; **C.** 13, 66, 66, 64; **D.** 84, 48, 44, 63; **E.** 99, 96, 93, 62

Page 40: A. 90, 70, 91, 72, 110; **B.** 84, 100, 192, 161, 112; **C.** 78, 312, 220, 204, 117; **D.** 252, 270, 288, 112, 56; **E.** 210, 126, 154, 170, 141; **F.** 38, 198, 336, 252, 415

Page 41: A. 2,488; 496, 900, 849, 1,998; 548; **B.** 1,001; 645, 824, 750, 927, 832; **C.** 3,609; 840, 756, 1,200; 888; 3,647; **D.** 3,699; 3,102; 864, 648, 408; 3,570; **E.** 6,349; 970, 2,439; 5,632; 672; 1,175; **F.** 1,086; 1,000; 1,688; 5,346; 963; 3,950

Page 42: A. $36.50, $27.28, $24.72, $43.05; **B.** $1.36, $7.92, $21.72, $14.95; **C.** $9.59, $8.19, $32.00, $11.07; **D.** $0.88, $11.46, $2.96, $47.60

Page 43: A. five groups of two circled, 2; **B.** three groups of five circled, 5; **C.** three groups of two circled, 2; **D.** two groups of four circled, 4; **E.** three groups of three circled, 3; **F.** four groups of three circled, 3; **G.** six groups of two circled, 2; **H.** three groups of six circled, 6; **I.** seven groups of two circled, 2

Page 44: All groups in each problem should have an equal number of objects drawn. **A.** 21 ÷ 3 = 7; **B.** 30 ÷ 5 = 6; **C.** 36 ÷ 9 = 4; **D.** 18 ÷ 6 = 3

Page 45: All groups in each problem should have the same number of objects drawn. **A.** 3; **B.** 4; **C.** 3; **D.** 4; **E.** 2; **F.** 6

Page 46: A. 6, 6, 7, 9; **B.** 7, 7, 9, 9; **C.** 7, 9, 9, 7; **D.** 6, 4, 8, 6; **E.** 4, 7, 5, 8; **F.** 4, 6, 5, 6; **G.** 7, 8, 4, 8; **H.** 8, 3, 9, 9

Page 47: A. 7 r1, 5 r2, 4 r3, 3 r4; **B.** 6 r1, 3 r3, 3 r2, 5 r3; **C.** 7 r7, 9 r1, 5 r1, 4 r4; **D.** 4 r2, 2 r1, 3 r1, 6 r2; **E.** 4 r1, 3 r4, 4 r6, 4 r6; **F.** 3 r4, 2 r4, 2 r1, 5 r2

Page 48: A. 3, 3, 3, 4, 4; **B.** 8, 7, 7, 8, 7; **C.** 6 r1, 3 r3, 3 r3, 3 r1, 3 r2; **D.** 6 r1, 5 r4, 3 r1, 5 r2, 8 r2; **E.** 9, 6, 8, 6, 6; **F.** 7 r1, 11 r4, 3 r2, 9 r3, 5 r1

Page 49: A. 4, 4; **B.** 3, 3; **C.** 4, 4; **D.** 5, 5; **E.** 5, 5; **F.** 3, 3; **G.** 3, 3; **H.** 6, 6; **I.** 5, 5; **J.** 9, 9; **K.** 5, 5; **L.** 2, 2; **M.** 4, 4; **N.** 2, 2; **O.** 6, 6

Page 50: Answers may be in a different order. **A.** 6 x 7 = 42, 7 x 6 = 42, 42 ÷ 7 = 6, 42 ÷ 6 = 7; **B.** 4 x 5 = 20, 5 x 4 = 20, 20 ÷ 5 = 4, 20 ÷ 4 = 5; **C.** 9 x 8 = 72, 8 x 9 = 72, 72 ÷ 8 = 9, 72 ÷ 9 = 8; **D.** 7 x 8 = 56, 8 x 7 = 56, 56 ÷ 8 = 7, 56 ÷ 7 = 8

Page 51: A. 48, 21, 16, 36, 14; **B.** 36, 24, 16, 12, 15; **C.** 64, 30, 6, 28, 18; **D.** 30, 56, 20, 49, 72; **E.** 9, 5, 8, 8; **F.** 9, 6, 7, 7; **G.** 8, 6, 3, 7; **H.** 5, 9, 8, 4

Page 52: A. 6:30, 11:00, 5:00; **B.** 6:00, 12:30, 10:30

Page 53: A. 30, 10:00, 10:30; **B.** 15, 2:00, 2:15; **C.** 35, 7:00, 7:35; **D.** 55, 9:00, 9:55; **E.** 10, 8:00, 8:10; **F.** 50, 4:00, 4:50; **G.** 5, 10:00, 10:05; **H.** 45, 6:00, 6:45; **I.** 30, 5:00, 5:30; **J.** 5, 12:00, 12:05

Answer Key

Page 54:

A.   B.

C.   D.

E.   F.

G.   H.

I.

Page 55: A. 82¢; **B.** 43¢; **C.** 95¢; **D.** 81¢; **E.** 85¢; **F.** 86¢; **G.** 29¢; **H.** 45¢

Page 56: A. 25, 50, 60, 70, 80, 90, 95, 100, 100; **B.** 50, 60, 65, 70, 75, 76, 77, 78, 78; **C.** 50, 60, 70, 80, 85, 90, 91, 92, 92; **D.** 25, 50, 60, 65, 70, 75, 76, 77, 77; **E.** 50, 75, 80, 85, 86, 87, 88, 89, 89; **F.** 25, 50, 75, 85, 90, 95, 100, 101, 101

Page 57: A. $1.55; **B.** $2.48; **C.** $7.45; **D.** $10.85; **E.** $17.17; **F.** $33.22

Page 58: A. $3.90; **B.** $3.80; **C.** $4.05; **D.** $5.40; **E.** $0.50; **F.** $4.05; **G.** $0.85; **H.** $15.00; **I.** $0.81; **J.** $0.05; **K.** $2.51; **L.** $0.77

Page 59: A. 6 feet; **B.** 9 inches; **C.** 1 inch; **D.** 20 inches; **E.** 2 inches; **F.** 1 inch; **G.** 2, 2, 1, 1, 6 inches

Page 60: A. 1, 24, 4; **B.** 12, 1, 6; **C.** 36, 2, 2; **D.** 200, 4,000, 3; **E.** <, >; **F.** <, >; **G.** <, =; **H.** =, >

Page 61: from left to right and top to bottom: 2 ounces, 5 grams, 18 kilograms, 105 pounds, 38 ounces, 26 pounds

Page 62: A. <, =, >; **B.** <, <, <; **C.** =, >, =; **D.** 85, 30, Answers will vary, but accept any answers that include warm-weather attire.; **E.** 32, 0, Answers will vary, but accept any answers that include cold-weather attire.

Page 63: A. $\frac{1}{6}$; **B.** $\frac{3}{8}$; **C.** $\frac{3}{4}$; **D.** $\frac{5}{8}$; **E.** $\frac{7}{9}$; **F.** $\frac{7}{12}$

Page 64: A. 2, 3, 12, 15; **B.** 2, 3, 16, 5; **C.** 4, 9, 8, 15; **D.** 8, 12, Answers will vary; **E.** 8, 9, 28, 28; **F.** 16, 15, 42, 8

Page 65: A. $\frac{1}{3} < \frac{2}{3}$; **B.** $\frac{2}{4} = \frac{4}{8}$; **C.** $\frac{3}{8} < \frac{1}{2}$; **D.** $\frac{1}{3} = \frac{2}{6}$; **E.** $\frac{3}{4} > \frac{2}{4}$; **F.** $\frac{1}{2} < \frac{3}{4}$

Page 66: A. $\frac{3}{4}$, $\frac{2}{8}$, $\frac{4}{5}$; **B.** $\frac{9}{10}$, $\frac{2}{8}$, $\frac{6}{10}$; **C.** $\frac{8}{9}$, $\frac{78}{100}$, $\frac{4}{12}$

Page 67: A. $4\frac{2}{3}$, $2\frac{2}{5}$, $4\frac{1}{4}$, $6\frac{1}{2}$; **B.** $1\frac{5}{7}$, $3\frac{3}{5}$, $6\frac{3}{4}$, $4\frac{3}{5}$; **C.** $3\frac{2}{3}$, $3\frac{3}{4}$, $4\frac{4}{5}$, $6\frac{1}{3}$; **D.** $9\frac{2}{4}$, $8\frac{2}{8}$, $7\frac{2}{6}$, $9\frac{3}{9}$; **E.** $2\frac{2}{8}$, $4\frac{2}{6}$, $6\frac{3}{6}$, $5\frac{2}{8}$

Page 68: A. 0.5, 1.4, 2.8, 3.7; **B.** 4.1, 5.8, 6.3, 7.9; **C.** 0.1, 0.7, 1.3, 1.6; **D.** 0.3, 0.8, 1.9, 2.4; **E.** 0.5, 2.8, 3.1, 3.6; **F.** 0.9, 1.4, 2.1, 2.6, 2.8

Page 69: blue: 0.8, 0.1, 0.7, 0.6, 0.4, 0.9; **green:** 0.15, 0.73, 0.36, 0.81

Page 70: A. 8.2, 3.8, 4.3; **B.** 9.77, 5.18, 7.7; **C.** 9.45, 6.4, 1.5; **D.** 7.84, 2.22, 2.16, 8.7, 7.6

Page 71: A. 0.3, 0.5, 0.9, 0.2; **B.** 0.8, 0.4, 0.7, 0.6; **C.** $\frac{6}{10}$, $\frac{4}{10}$, $\frac{7}{10}$, $\frac{8}{10}$; **D.** $\frac{3}{10}$, $\frac{5}{10}$, $\frac{2}{10}$, $\frac{9}{10}$; **E.** $\frac{13}{10}$, $1\frac{3}{10}$, 1.3; **F.** $\frac{16}{10}$, $1\frac{6}{10}$, 1.6; **G.** $\frac{18}{10}$, $1\frac{8}{10}$, 1.8; **H.** $\frac{20}{20}$, 2, 2.0

Page 72: A. 7, $\frac{7}{10}$, 0.7; **B.** 2, $\frac{2}{10}$, 0.2; **C.** 5, $\frac{5}{10}$, 0.5; **D.** 4, $\frac{4}{10}$, 0.4; **E.** 3, $\frac{3}{10}$, 0.3; **F.** 8, $\frac{8}{10}$, 0.8; **G.** 9, $\frac{9}{10}$, 0.9; **H.** 6, $\frac{6}{10}$, 0.6; **I.** 10, $\frac{10}{10}$, 1.0, The whole box should be shaded.

Page 73: A. 1, 0, 7; **B.** 5, 6, 0; **C.** 3, 9, 1; **D.** 16, 0, 6; **E.** 0, 1, 3; **F.** 7, 9, 3; **G.** 3, 0, 1; **H.** 1, 2, 5; **I.** 4, 1, 1; **J.** 2, 5, 3; **K.** 9, 1, 0; **L.** 8, 8, 4; **M.** 1.80

N. 3.2

O. 4.2

P. 3.07

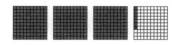

Q. 4.23

Summer Bridge Math RB-904087

Answer Key

Page 74:

A.

B.

C.

D.

E.

F.

Page 75: A. 3, 6, 9, 12, 15, 18, 21, 24, 27, 30, 33, 36, 39, 42, 45, 48, 51, 54, 57, 60, 63, 66, 69, 72, 75, 78, 81, 84, 87, 90, 93, 96, 99; **B.** 4, 8, 12, 16, 20, 24, 28, 32, 36, 40, 44, 48, 52, 56, 60, 64, 68, 72, 76, 80, 84, 88, 92, 96, 100; **C.** 6, 12, 18, 24, 30, 36, 42, 48, 54, 60, 66, 72, 78, 84, 90, 96; **D.** 11, 22, 33, 44, 55, 66, 77, 88, 99; Answers about patterns will vary.

Page 76: A. 13, 15, 17; **B.** 13, 16, 19, 22; **C.** 26, 31, 36, 41; **D.** 14, 18, 22, 26; **E.** [ ] x 3 – 6

Page 77: A. square, rhombus, rectangle, trapezoid; **B.** square or rhombus; **C.** triangle; **D.** circle; **E.** pentagon; **F.** hexagon; **G.** octagon; **H.** square, rhombus, rectangle, hexagon, trapezoid, octagon; **I.** Answers will vary but

may include a trapezoid has one pair of parallel sides, but a rhombus has two pairs of parallel sides.

Page 78: A. cone, 1; **B.** cylinder, 2; **C.** sphere, 0; **D.** rectangular prism, 6; **E.** pyramid, 5; **F.** cube, 6; **G.** cylinder, 2; **H.** sphere, 0; **I.** pyramid, 5; **J.** cone, 1; **K.** rectangular prism, 6

Page 79: Lines of symmetry should be drawn correctly.

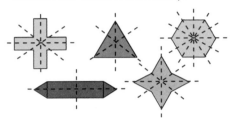

Page 80: A. 24 units; **B.** 10 units; **C.** 24 inches; **D.** 16 cm; **E.** 21 miles; **F.** 32 miles

Page 81: A. equal; **B.** equal; **C.** none; **D.** 3; **E.** 3

Page 82: A. the times and channels of Wednesday night television programs; **B.** 8:30 P.M.; **C.** 5; **D.** *Eating Right*; **E.** 2 hours; **F.** 4; **G.** 5; **H.** Answers will vary.

Page 83: A. 5°; **B.** 5°; **C.** 50; **D.** 10°; **E.** **F.** **G.**

H. (1, 1), (0, 4)

Page 84: A. 5 pots; **B.** 6 boxes; **C.** 7 cards; **D.** 11 fish; **E.** 9 pieces of candy; **F.** 13 books

Page 85: A. 109 pennies; **B.** 1,221 cans; **C.** 233 televisions; **D.** 13 pounds; **E.** 1,811 books; **F.** 88 points

Page 86: A. 102 miles; **B.** 336 pages; **C.** 250 trading cards; **D.** 292 stamps

Page 87: A. 72 seeds; **B.** 102 bugs; **C.** $8.00; **D.** 91 coins; **E.** 32 honks; **F.** 48 spoons of powdered mix

Page 88: A. 6 toys; **B.** 3 papers; **C.** 6 cookies; **D.** 22 horses

Page 89: A. 4, 2; **B.** 7, 1; **C.** 2, 1; **D.** 6, 1

Page 90: A. 37 minutes; **B.** 9:00 P.M.; **C.** 7 minutes; **D.** 8:47 P.M.; **E.** 1 hour and 21 minutes; **F.** 3 hours

Page 91: A. $22.22; **B.** $4.27; **C.** $17.50; **D.** $34.00; **E.** $32.00; **F.** $12.00

Page 92: A. 20 minutes; **B.** 18 hours

© Rainbow Bridge Publishing